HABITAT GARDEN

HABITAT GARDEN

PETER GRANT

Permissions

'Possum' and 'Sister Spider' by James Charlton, published in *Luminous Bodies*, Montpelier Press, Hobart, 2002, reproduced with the kind permission of the author.

'Birth of a Naturalist' by Louise Fabiani, published in *The Green Alembic*, Signal Editions, Montreal, 1999, reproduced with the kind permission of the author.

'Waterlog' by Roger Deakin, published by Chatto & Windus, London 1999, reproduced with the kind permission of the author.

Published by ABC Books for the
AUSTRALIAN BROADCASTING CORPORATION
GPO Box 9994 Sydney NSW 2001

Copyright © Australian Broadcasting Corporation 2003

First published September 2003
Reprinted July 2006

All rights reserved. No part of this publication may be reproduced, stored in a retrieval system or transmitted in any form or by any means, electronic, mechanical, photocopying, recording or otherwise, without the prior written permission of the Australian Broadcasting Corporation.

ISBN 10: 0 7333 1279 9
ISBN 13: 978 07333 12793

Designed and typeset by Mega City Design
Illustrations by Nives Porcellato and Andy Craig
All photographs by the author unless otherwise credited
Set in Berkeley 11/14
Colour reproduction by Pageset, Melbourne
Printed and bound in China by Everbest Printing

5 4 3 2

To my amazing wife, Lynne, who so often practises in the garden while I preach. And to my late father, Donald M Grant, who would have been surprised – and hopefully delighted – to see his thumbs inherited at last.

Foreword

If I and other landscapers had access to this book when we were planting 'native' gardens in the 1960s and 1970s, Australian gardens today might look very different. My first gardens were planted with exotics, many of which are now considered weeds and have invaded the bush. The prevailing concept of the Australian landscape was very different: the huge arid and semi-arid areas of the continent were regarded as 'gaba country' – Great Australian Bugger All.

Then came a movement of some awakening. Arthur Boyd, Sidney Nolan and many other painters asked us to see the landscape differently; Patrick White and Judith Wright were writing about it; and architects began designing houses that blended with the landscape and suited Australian conditions – they and their clients wanted native gardens. Gardeners made more blunders. Anything that was Australian was 'native' and we selected plants from out of area – many of which would also become invasive weeds. That movement lost impetus, though native planting in parks and along freeways continued.

Now we are learning to use indigenous species – plants that are or were local to where we live. In his timely book, *Habitat Garden*, Peter Grant presents sound gardening reasons for planting local. Crucial to this are the interlocking reasons of aesthetics and ecology – the need to recognise that this continent is not antipodean Europe or Asia.

Everything is connected to everything else. Drought, salinity, the loss of plant and animal species, has caught up with us and forced our hand. Although we can still walk the length of most streets in most Australian cities and not see a native garden or a native plant, more of us value our country, and wish to connect with it. Peter shows us how we can do this in our own gardens with less effort and expense than planting an exotic garden, but with a huge contribution to our flora, fauna, and the whole interconnected thing.

Habitat Garden is a practical guide. To start, Peter suggests taking weekend strolls around nearby bush to see what we might recreate or what plants we can use. He also explains why we might want to plant local, what the benefits are, and how to do it. The principles are applicable anywhere in Australia, and simple.

As local plants grow, the local food-chain begins to re-form. Nectar, pollen, fruits, invertebrates and insects multiply, birds return. In some areas, some frogs, reptiles and mammals can reappear. We all live in a habitat, let us make ours as rich as we can.

As individuals we cannot, in one or two years, correct our country's macrocosmic problems such as salinity and erosion. But, in that time – and within our own microcosms – we can establish a local native garden which will be used by native fauna. Let us not underestimate the worth of such action.

BARY DOWLING
Author and nature columnist, *The Age*
May 2003

Acknowledgements

Many people have assisted in the creation of this book through their advice, example and research. I would particularly like to thank:

- my colleagues at the Tasmanian Parks and Wildlife Service, past and present, including Ian Marmion, Glenys Jones, Raymond Brereton, Chris Corbett, Sib Corbett, Peter Brown, Sylvia Outridge, Mick Ilowski, Wendy Basire, Nicole Sheriff, Louise Gilfedder, Jenni Burdon and Andrew Smith;
- my daughter Sally Oakley, for her generous assistance with research;
- Mark Fountain of the Royal Tasmanian Botanical Gardens for his invaluable advice;
- colleagues associated with Greening Australia, including Mark and Lyn Butz, Louise Bull, Jim Robinson, Sue Streatfield and Melissa Horgan;
- Ian Jeanneret and Peter Tonelli for their fabulous photography and great company in the bush;
- Mary Knights for sewing the seed, Helen Cushing of ABC Gardening Australia for watering and tending the seedling, and Brigitta Doyle and Jo Mackay of ABC Books for bringing it to harvest;
- and the many other individuals, from researchers and practitioners to poets and writers, who allowed me to benefit from their labours. At the risk of missing out some, I include: Valerie Close, Tom Mumbray, Louise Fabiani, James Charlton, Roger Deakin, Gordon Rowland, Robin MacGillivray, Kerrie Heatley and Keith Corbett.

The shortcomings of the book are mine, but each of you has improved it in numerous ways.

Contents

Foreword   vii
Acknowledgements   viii

Chapter 1. Introduction   1
    What is a habitat garden?   2
    Why habitat gardens?   2

Chapter 2. Planning your habitat garden   5
    A different ethos: the basic principles of habitat gardening   5
    Why plan?   12
    The planning process   12
    Some habitat garden scenarios   14

Chapter 3. Growing your habitat garden   17
    Propagation   17
    Direct seeding of native plants for larger gardens   29
    Plantings around eucalypts   31

Chapter 4. Maintaining your habitat garden   33
    Water and habitat gardening   33
    Mulching   34
    Bush rocks in the habitat garden   37
    Pruning native plants   37
    Managing weeds and pests   38
    Threats to the habitat garden   41
    Changing with your habitat garden   43

Chapter 5.	Bringing life to your habitat garden	45
	Birds	45
	Mammals	51
	Insects and other invertebrates	58
	Amphibians	65
	Reptiles	69
	Aquatic animals	71
Chapter 6.	Special cases – habitat gardening in difficult zones	77
	Coastal gardens	77
	Rainforest gardens	78
	Arid and semi-arid gardens	80
	Alpine and cool climate gardens	81
Chapter 7.	Getting help	85
	Government/community environmental care groups	85
	Specialist gardens	85
	Societies and clubs	88
	Specialist nurseries	89
	Further reading	89

Afterword	90
Index	91

1. Introduction

Everything lives in a habitat. Whether it's a rat up a drain or an earwig in a cornstalk, all living things, humans included, depend on a complex network of other living things, as well as air, water, earth, sunlight and shelter. Yet most humans live in a highly modified habitat. We can spend all day in a building with artificial light and air conditioning. We can travel inside vehicles, eat packaged food and amuse ourselves with electronic gadgetry. We can sometimes forget that there's an outside world, or can even begin to think that we aren't a part of the natural environment.

Gardens have long reminded us that we are part of life on earth. A garden can help reconnect us with the soil, the air, the sun and the rain, the things that are essential to all life on earth – including our own. In the truest sense gardening is a recreation – both recreating something and enjoying something.

The habitat garden is about reclaiming our connection with the environment, starting literally in our own backyards. Every backyard is part of the larger environment, and every backyard provides a habitat, a particular native environment, for something, whether we like it or not.

Even a concrete balcony may provide a suitable environment for, say, algae or spiders. Habitat gardening is about getting involved in choosing what comes to our

A dewy web – a beautiful sight, even for arachnophobes, and a sign of a healthy habitat.

backyard to live or visit. The key to working out and identifying natural habitats is to look and listen and then work on developing that habitat, even if it is encouraging algae or spiders

What is a habitat garden?

A habitat garden is simply a garden that attempts to favour certain types of spaces for certain types of plants, animals, insects and other life forms. In Australia that means a garden that favours Australian native plants over plants from other countries, and Australian life forms and communities over those from any other place. More than that a habitat garden favours *local* plants and *local* communities over those from anywhere else.

Habitats are complex things and involve an intricate interconnection of everything from bacteria, bugs and rocks to sunshine, water and temperature. No-one should pretend that they are going to be able to re-create a complete and wholesome natural habitat in the average backyard. But a habitat garden can start to recreate some of the spaces that we've squeezed out of our local environments in recent years.

Why habitat gardens?

Few things are as rewarding as getting to know your local flora and fauna. To sit at a window and watch a honeyeater hovering over a Grevillea that you've planted, or to wander in your garden and spot a bandicoot sneaking back under a bush, these are some of the enduring pleasures that can be part of every habitat gardener's day. And the opportunity to watch the changes that come with the seasons: the effect of good rains, the blossoming of wattle, the first flight of newly winged cicadas, or the return of migratory birds.

There's more than personal pleasure involved when considering a habitat garden. Have you looked around suburbia lately? Have you been out in the bush that you used to play in as a child? More and more of our country is being covered by concrete and housing developments, roads and shopping malls. Most of the bush that gets used in this way ends up being alienated from its natural inhabitants, if it isn't destroyed totally. The environment that had supported a vastly complex web of plants and animals ends up being simplified for human use, often with no thought of what becomes of the other life forms that used to call it home.

It doesn't have to be this way. The kinds of alterations, that we call development, to the natural environment can, and sometimes do, carefully take into account its natural inhabitants. Housing or industrial developments can be designed with habitat preservation in mind.

Even in established housing areas, habitat gardening is one way we can play a small part in restoring our environment. Australia is one of the driest countries on Earth, with generally shallow, nutrient-poor soils, so our gardening style can have a significant impact on the environment, for good or ill. For example, if we persist with gardening styles that are based on the cooler, wetter climates of places like Europe, we use enormous amounts of water and artificial nutrients. This type of gardening not only uses up personal energy but also precious natural resources. Habitat gardening offers the chance to find a gardening style that's better suited to our climate and soil conditions.

Another argument for habitat gardening relates to the sobering fact that since the European takeover, Australia's native plants and animals have become rare or extinct at a much higher rate than almost anywhere else on Earth. We've introduced hard-hoofed animals, such as sheep and cattle, that graze and trample in ways that native animals don't. Added to that are the plant and insect pests we've let loose all over the country, and it's clear that we've drastically changed our natural environment. To put it simply, we've shrunk the number of habitats available for our native plants and animals.

Of course Australia has a wonderful array of national parks and nature reserves which provide havens for some of our flora and fauna, but such reserves only cover about 6 per cent of our land area. Often national parks are on land that was otherwise considered marginal for productive purposes. Because these parks do not represent the full spectrum of ecosystems, reserves alone can never provide enough habitat for healthy populations of the amazing diversity of life that calls Australia home.

What's needed is a popular movement among landholders of all sorts, even suburban ones. It's a movement that aims to retain the wonderful range of unique species, the biodiversity, of our island continent.

We already see vast tree planting and bush regeneration efforts from governments as well as from local groups and organisations such as Bushcare, Landcare and Greening Australia. Individual farmers and farming organisations all over Australia are also making huge efforts. Habitat gardening brings people power to home gardening. It is the next wave, the green revolution brought into the humble backyards of Australia.

Habitat gardening has a modest but potentially profound aim – to try and win back some space in our backyards for the disappearing Australians, our local native plants and animals. The aim of this book is to help you, wherever you are in Australia, to design and grow your own habitat garden so that you too can contribute to this down-to-earth revolution.

2. Planning your habitat garden

Before you set spade to soil or set foot inside a garden centre, even before you start planning your garden, there are some basic principles of habitat gardening that come before everything else. They will help determine much of what you end up doing in your garden.

A different ethos: the basic principles of habitat gardening
Principle 1: Favouring the locals

It is absolutely basic to habitat gardening that you are trying to restore, protect or recreate the kinds of habitats that once covered your local area. This means planting your garden with species that once thrived, and perhaps still do thrive, in your local area. The thinking behind this is straightforward. The lifeforms that naturally live locally, from invertebrates to frogs and birds to mammals, have developed alongside the plant, soil and water conditions that exist locally. These are the species that are going to benefit the most from a local habitat garden, or be harmed most by the continuing removal of local bush.

It's vital to the creation of an authentic habitat garden that you get to know the locals and find out what is indigenous to your local area. If you feel you lack the expertise, help is never far away. Many councils keep lists of indigenous plants and plant nurseries are often a great source of information, as well as local plants, provided they have some interest and expertise in local flora. There may also be a Landcare (or similar) group which can provide information about plants and animals in your neighbourhood. Radio gardening shows and local newspaper columns can also be helpful.

In urban fringe areas and other places where some natural bushland remains, you may choose to find out some of this information yourself. Start by taking a couple of weekend strolls around the nearby bush. Try looking for:
- natural or semi-natural bushland;
- native and local plants that appear to grow well in the area;
- evidence of native animals (birds, mammals, insects, reptiles, amphibians);
- the types of soils, rocks, trees and other basic habitat niches that are available for native animals;
- any natural corridors that already seem to provide ways for animals to move around your neighbourhood;

What does 'local' mean?

In parts of Australia, where there is little change in soil, climate, slope or aspect, the term 'local' might extend over hundreds of square kilometres. Elsewhere significant changes in ecotypes can occur within a matter of 50m. What is local to your garden is going to depend on how quickly and significantly conditions change in your area. As a rule of thumb 'local' can be considered any area within, say, 50km in which conditions are comparable with those in your area.

- any particular threats to native flora and fauna such as lots of cats or dogs, or feral pests;
- other factors that might limit birds or animals in your area; for example, limited sources of clean water.

Looking locally should help you find out which native plant and animal species you might expect in your garden, once you get the garden going. By observing carefully and doing some research on what you find, the end result should be a garden that is enticing to local animals.

Far from restricting the kind of garden you will end up with, using local species will give you the opportunity to celebrate *all* of your local species, animals as well as plants. Given that there are over 800 different species of *Acacia* and a similar number of eucalypts in Australia (just two examples), there are sure to be some favourite native species that you can find in your area.

Favouring locals will help you think about the use of introduced plants and materials. That's not to say they're out altogether. Few people have 100 per cent habitat gardens because many of us want to grow plants for other practical and aesthetic reasons, whether it's lemon trees for their fruit or exotic annuals for cut flowers. Being aware of the danger of garden escapes, that is, plants that move out of our gardens to become the source of so many of the weeds that infest our natural bushland, is half the battle. Vigilance and hard work can take care of the rest.

Principle 2: Mimicking nature

Natural habitats are amazingly complex and multi-layered. Those who describe the dry interior of Australia as 'featureless' or 'empty', 'unchanging for mile after mile' only need to open their eyes. Even a desert is full of change and complexity. Another term for that complexity is *biodiversity*. The successful habitat gardener needs to be aware of the complexity of local habitats. This involves knowing what is local and then introducing or nurturing habitats that are going to favour those locals. In essence, mimicking nature and natural habitats will help protect the biodiversity of the local area.

One way to help you consider biodiversity is to look at your garden from the ground up. Layers become the key factor. For example, an average suburban garden is made up of the following layers:
- the soil;
- the soil covering, such as mulch, leaf litter, etcetera;
- other ground features, such as rocks or fallen logs;
- places that hold water;
- ground-covering plants;
- shrubs and under-storey plants;
- trees.

> **Look, don't take!**
>
> Looking locally doesn't mean 'taking locally'. Remember you are trying to preserve or increase niches and habitats for local life. Taking plants, rocks, soil, leaf-litter etc. from the bush for your garden not only defeats the purpose – it may also be against the law. Look so you can learn, but leave the bush intact for the local plants and animals.

Each of these individual layers is a full and intricate area of study in itself. A simple and useful technique is to think of the layers from a bird's point of view. An insect-eating bird such as a Tawny Frogmouth looks for insects, spiders and small mammals in and around wooded areas. It uses trees as watchtowers, often coming to the ground at night to eat or to drink. In searching for its prey it may scratch through mulch or leaf litter. It generally nests in mature trees. For the frogmouth mature trees and an insect-rich forest floor are the crucial layers.

Contrast this with a nectar-eating bird such as a New Holland Honeyeater. It requires flowers for the nectar, but eats insects as well. It also needs ample foliage for nesting and for protection from enemies such as predatory birds or cats. A skilled flyer that can catch what it needs on the wing means that it will rarely come to the ground. For this honeyeater, the shrubs and the trees, the middle layers are the important ones.

Even though the 'bird's eye view' technique is an over-simplification, it illustrates how complex a healthy habitat garden can become. Add amphibians, reptiles, mammals, spiders and insects into the frame and you increase that complexity. But that, is exactly what you're trying to do, to see your garden as an extension or a simulation of the biodiversity of natural habitats.

Principle 3: Watching your water

Australia may be the driest inhabited continent on earth but most of us live in the well-watered parts, far from the 'wide

(continued page 11)

Every garden provides a habitat for something. Adding layers of complexity increases the diversity of life in your garden.

An example of layered planting

Using plants suited to many parts of Australia. Where necessary adapt for your local area. Use only local native species as some introduced native varieties can become invasive.

Grasses and groundcovers	Description/habitat benefits
Themeda species (kangaroo grass)	Provides food, seeds for birds and stems for caterpillars and shelter for lizards and frogs.
Chionochloa pallida (wallaby grass) (formerly *Danthonia*)	Provides food for birds and caterpillars. Moth larvae feed on roots.
Ehrharta stipoides (weeping grass)	Provides food for Common Brown Ringlet Butterfly's caterpillars as well as seeds for birds.
Correa species	Flowers are rich in nectar, attracting birds and invertebrates, including butterflies.
Goodenia species	Yellow flowers attract invertebrates which, in turn, feed birds.
Scaevola species (fan flowers)	Insects are attracted to the nectar of the flowers.
Hibbertia species (guinea flowers)	Flowers provide food for a wide range of birds and invertebrates. Some varieties are good climbers and can be used in different habitat layers.
Commelina cyanea (native wandering jew)	Provides shelter for lizards and frogs.

Tufting and clumping plants	Description/habitat benefits
Lomandra species (sagg, mat rushes)	Attracts birds, insect larvae and other invertebrates. Provides shelter and nesting sites for birds, reptiles and small mammals.
Dianella species (flax lilies)	Berries provide food for birds and invertebrates.
Gahnia species (sword grass, saw sedge)	Some larvae (for example, Sword-grass Brown Butterfly) feed on the foliage. Provides good shelter for small animals and invertebrates.
Juncus species (rushes)	Attracts seed- and fruit-eating birds and invertebrates. Provides good shelter and a lookout for many water-loving creatures.
Poa species (tussock grasses)	Seeds attract birds. Provides shelter and nesting sites for birds, reptiles and small mammals.
Carex species (sedges)	Provides refuge for frogs and invertebrates. Suitable for the edges of garden pond or other moist sites.

An example of layered planting (cont.)

Climbers

	Description/habitat benefits
Clematis species	Flowers attract butterflies and other invertebrates. The bushes are ideal for nesting birds.
Hardenbergia violacea (false sarsaparilla)	Attracts seed- and fruit-eating birds and invertebrates. Good for refuge and nesting sites.
Kennedia species (coral peas)	Pea-like flowers attract nectar feeders, including birds, butterflies and moths. Seeds and feeding insects also attract birds.

Shrubs and bushes

	Description/habitat benefits
Acacia species, particularly small local wattle species	Blossoms attract butterflies and other invertebrates; seeds provide food for birds. Dense foliage and broken limbs offer shelter and nesting sites for a variety of birds and mammals. Borers attack the wood and attract insect-feeding birds.
Grevillea species	Flowers attract nectar-feeding birds and invertebrates which, in turn, attract insect-feeding birds.
Bursaria spinosa (blackthorn, sweet bursaria)	Scented flowers attract a variety of butterflies and other invertebrates.
Pultenaea species (bacon and eggs, bush pea)	Flowers attract birds and invertebrates; seeds attract birds. Spiky foliage is ideal for sheltering and nesting birds.
Olearia species (daisy bushes)	Flowers attract butterflies and other invertebrates.
Prostanthera species (mint bushes)	Popular for fragrant foliage, though flowers also attract nectar-feeding birds and invertebrates.
Banksia species	Flowers are a food source for birds, invertebrates and small mammals. (Use varieties that are local to your area.)
Callistemon species (bottlebrushes)	Hugely attractive to nectar-feeding birds and invertebrates. (Use varieties that are local to your area.)
Calytrix species (fringe myrtles)	Flowers attract butterflies and other invertebrates.
Hakea species	Flowers attract nectar-feeding birds and invertebrates. Dense, prickly foliage offers good shelter and nesting.
Kunzea species	Flowers attract nectar-feeding birds and invertebrates. Bushes provide good shelter.

An example of layered planting (cont.)

Shrubs and bushes	Description/habitat benefits
Leptospermum species (tea trees)	Flowers attract butterflies, other invertebrates and some birds. In some the varieties foliage is good for shelter and nesting.
Melaleuca species (paperbarks)	Flowers attract nectar-feeding birds and invertebrates, which in turn attract insect-feeding birds.

Trees	Description/habitat benefits
Eucalyptus species (gum trees) (see also *Corymbia* species)	No Australian habitat garden can be without gum trees! No matter which species occur in your area the chances are their flowers will attract birds and invertebrates; their branches and trunks will provide shelter or nesting for a huge variety of bird, mammal and invertebrate life; their fallen limbs will offer ground shelter for lizards and invertebrates. Beware of choosing tall eucalypts in small or medium gardens (see box p. 27)
Allocasuarina species (she-oaks)	Attract seed- and fruit-eating birds; good for nesting; fallen 'leaves' (branchlets) make a good mulch.
Acacia (small local wattle species)	Blossoms attract butterflies and other invertebrates; seeds are food for birds; dense foliage and broken limbs offer shelter and nesting sites for a variety of birds and mammals. Borers attack wood and attract insect-feeding birds. Fallen limbs offer ground shelter for lizards and invertebrates.
Callitris species (cypress pines)	Seeds attract parrots and similar birds; dense foliage good for shelter and nesting of birds and mammals.
Melicope elleryana (formerly Euodia)	For warmer parts of Australia. Best known as the food plant of the Superb Blue Ulysses Butterfly (*Papilio Ulysses*) in Queensland. Fruit also attract birds.
Syzygium species (lilly pillies)	Generally for warmer parts of Australia. Fruit attracts birds and bats; flowers attract nectar-feeding birds and invertebrates; foliage is good for shelter and nesting.

brown land' of Dorothea Mackellar's poem. Add a couple of taps per garden and it's easy for us to imagine that dry weather and droughts are no threat to our gardens. The temptation is to grow whatever we want, regardless of how much water is required.

Habitat gardeners tend to think carefully about this. The fact is that much of our native vegetation, even in wetter areas, has developed against a background of dry weather and/or impoverished soils. Overwatering can develop a healthy-looking garden, but it will also lead to artificiality by encouraging species which flourish with water, and discouraging drought-tolerant species.

If the aim is to copy a natural habitat, too much water will create a different kind of habitat. Of course, there are other reasons for watching water in the habitat garden. Some of these are economic: watering systems cost money to set up, and in many areas water rates are charged on a user-pays basis. Others are ecological: overuse of water in the garden might contribute to the inundation of far-away catchments for reservoirs, and the devastation of local ecology there, just so you and others can be supplied with more water than you really need. The overuse of water can also encourage the spread of weed species, and in some areas overwatering has contributed to serious increases in soil salinity.

Drip watering systems, which can distribute water to very specific areas, can be a good compromise. They use a fraction of the water of conventional sprinklers or hoses and only water the plants that need watering, such as vulnerable seedlings or trees in their early years. Using carefully chosen mulching material can also help to save water.

Principle 4: Managing pests and weeds naturally

Many of the principles of habitat gardening come from organic gardening. As with organic gardening the key is the creation of a healthy and dynamic ecosystem without the need to resort to the use of chemical herbicides and pesticides or artificial fertilisers. In such a system a single species is unlikely to gain dominance for long enough to become a pest because there is a healthy diversity of life. This biodiversity helps to create a balance between predator and prey.

Achieving this approximation of a

Three basic planning questions

1. What are you starting with?
This is not only about what's already planted in your garden, but also such issues such as soil types, slope, aspect and local climate.

2. What do you want to end up with?
Break this up into the major elements of the garden that you are seeking to create. For example, is attracting birds to your garden very important? Are water habitats to feature? Is it to be a child-friendly garden? Is it to be the whole garden, or only a section?

3. How are you going to get there?
What needs to happen? What are the main obstacles to be overcome? What sort of timeframe do you have? What about finances? Do you need to seek advice from a garden professional?

natural system is not always simple. Every garden of every description ends up with weeds and other pest species. The habitat gardener deals with these problems by a combination of means. These are spelled out in further in Chapter 4, but can be summarised as follows:
1. Using Integrated Pest Management
2. Developing a Tolerance for Damage

When considered with the four key principles in mind the planning of your habitat garden can begin.

Why plan?

Are the two following scenarios familiar? It's the weekend and you find yourself at the garden centre. There's a sale on and, unable to resist a bargain, you buy a car-boot load of plants, everything from seedlings to trees. You get them home and only then do you really start to think about where you're going to plant them all.

The other scenario finds you in your already established garden scratching your head. The garden was set out by someone else many years ago, and it reflects their priorities, not yours. You want to change that, but you don't want to tear down the whole garden, and especially the established trees.

In both cases the question is: where do you start? And in both cases the short answer is: planning. Short but not necessarily simple. If the idea of planning appears daunting, simplify it by asking yourself three simple questions.

The planning process

Gardening is part science and part art. Much of the joy of gardening comes from finding creative solutions to the challenges that you and every gardener faces. When planning a habitat garden, creative and lateral thinking is just as important as your research into local species and habitats. And because each garden is as unique as each gardener, it follows that there is no one way to create a habitat garden. In fact, there are hundreds of ways to be creative about this sort of gardening. To help get that creative planning underway, keep going back to the three basic questions.

1. What are you starting with?

Every gardener has to start with what they've got. Firstly there are what we might call *site factors*. These factors include geology, soil types, aspect and slope and they can subtly change from one part of the block to the next, altering what's possible in different parts of your garden. For instance, in southern parts of the country a sheltered north-facing nook in the garden may have a longer growing season than other parts of the garden. In drier parts of Australia a shaded gully may hold water longer and create a refuge for animals as well as plants.

It is also worth noting your local *climatic factors*. More than just your broad climate, this takes into account things like the *localised* temperature range and hours of sunshine, and local rainfall and wind effects.

In most cases you'll also need to consider *pre-existing factors*, that is the plants, buildings, paths, proximity of the garden to roads and other elements of the garden that are already in place. Where climatic and site factors can only be altered slightly, these pre-existing factors are usually open to change. Here's where planning starts to come into its own. You can cut down trees, remove paths, even take out buildings if you need to. In most cases there will also be some significant 'immovables'. Usually the house is one of these. The position of your house on the block will greatly effect the design of your garden, as will the positioning of any neighbouring buildings or boundary fences.

If you're starting with a bare bulldozed block, some other issues arise. These may include where to place your house and your services such as water pipes, sewerage, car access and power, and what to do about soil. Imported soil brings with it the risk of imported weed seeds as well as other introduced soil organisms. It will also alter the overall soil quality and habitat opportunities.

Having noted all of the significant elements that already exist in your garden, or that you want to change, put them down in a list or on a diagram/drawing. You could also photograph the garden and annotate the photos. Once that's done you're ready to move to stage two.

2. What do you end up with?

Here's where you can get your imagination running. What sort of habitat garden do you want to end up with? Will it take up the whole of the garden, or just a part? Will it have a water feature? Will it welcome mammals as well as birds and insects? The possibilities are virtually endless, and they're up to you to choose.

Here are some possible ways to help you decide on the type of habitat garden:

The natural look to strive for: bottlebrush and sagg beneath a stand of eucalyptus.

Planning your habitat garden 13

- walk around your garden, looking carefully as you go;
- take a photo or series of photos and study them, think about what will need to change;
- place tracing paper over your photos and sketch in the alterations you have in mind. Add and subtract features. You don't have to be a great artist to get some idea of how changes might look;
- use a digital camera and drawing software to go through a similar process on your computer;
- use a garden planning software package.

There's great benefit in simply getting to know your garden. Spend time in the garden at different hours of the day and night, and in all kinds of weather. It's surprising how different it can look and the different ideas that may arise, if you walk around your garden during a shower of rain or when there's a strong wind blowing. Once you've decided approximately what you want, you're ready to go to the next step.

3. How are you going to get there?

It's no use having grand plans if you don't have the know-how or the means to realise those plans. Time, money and other resources, such as access to willing helpers and/or machinery, are fairly crucial here. If money is short but you have some time and a willingness to learn, you can do it all yourself. You just have to set a flexible timetable to allow for learning time.

Most gardeners will choose to have a professional in for at least some of the more difficult tasks, for example, excavation and tree removal. If time is tighter than the budget you may choose to have a professional take over some of the other tasks, such as watering systems, garden planning and even plant selection.

Once you've worked out what you want to do in your garden, and who *else* is going to be involved, the rest largely comes down to technical issues. These include such things like propagation, planting techniques, mulching and watering. Again in the habitat garden these need to be approached slightly differently than other forms of gardening. Chapter 3 will cover these technical issues in more detail.

Some habitat garden scenarios
The bulldozed block – a habitat garden from scratch

On the outer fringes of ever-spreading suburbia, a young couple buys a quarter-acre block in a new subdivision. It has been completely cleared of all previous vegetation but the couple are keen to return it to a more natural state. They are excited that a gully with semi-natural bush is next to their block.

Once the services have all been completed, and the house site has been chosen and excavated, the couple start to plan their garden. First, they spend a lot of time on the block, in all weather, so they can get a feel for it. They notice that one side of the gently sloping block retains water more than the other, and that there seems to be a wet patch at the bottom of this part of the garden. They work out the orientation of the block, where the sun will shine best in winter, where the shade will be created by buildings and potential plantings.

The young couple also walk through the nearby bushland making a note of what grows and lives there. They contact the local council and learn that a Landcare group has just started work on restoring a nearby creek. They're told that the council has a nursery that can provide them with some local native species. Their local habitat education has begun, and when they combine that with their growing knowledge of conditions on their own block, their habitat garden will be all the better for it.

An evolving habitat garden

In this example the large front garden has some magnificent exotic trees, including liquid amber, scarlet oak and rhododendron, some of them are over 50 years old. Whatever is planted now, the gardener will never see anything of such grandeur in his lifetime. Rather than pull these exotics out, the gardener chooses to concentrate plantings of local native species in other parts of the garden, especially in the back garden as this section backs onto a reserve containing some remnant native bush.

The gardener also decides to replace older plants opportunistically, as they become old or die, with local native species. By doing this he is approaching habitat gardening as a process, with the eventual goal of having local species dominate, rather than pulling out all the existing plants and replacing them immediately, like a sudden takeover. It is a process of evolution rather than revolution. Even in its early stages, this patchwork garden of local and exotic species will still be of benefit to some animal species.

A habitat zone in a small formal garden

This small inner city property is in an area of dense, older-style housing. There is virtually no front garden. The back garden has lots of paving, a small amount of lawn, and a formal fountain in the middle of the garden. The only tree in the garden is a weeping bottlebrush hanging over a sandpit in the corner of the backyard.

The new owner's children have grown up, so she removes the sandpit. She identifies that the bottlebrush is a local native, and decides to create a zone of bird- and insect-attracting plants in the corner of the yard. Talking with the neighbours on that side of her garden, she finds that they want to attract birds too. Together they agree on a couple of different sorts of plants to put on either side of their boundary. They replace that section of fence with a trellis which they cover with a couple of native climbers. They also top the new fence with a birdbath on a catproof metal pole. After planting out some native grasses, a few low-growing flowering shrubs and another bottlebrush tree, all locally-occurring, they mulch and water the new patch. The owner then sits back to watch the honeyeaters, wrens, pardalotes and parrots.

Even as she relaxes in her new garden, this gardener has her eye on the fountain. She's beginning to think about how she might expand it into a water garden with frogs, native fish and local plants. One habitat zone may soon become two.

A wildlife corridor in a bushy area

A small acreage on the urban fringe has been cleared and sown out to pasture for many years. There's a grove of fruit trees down one side of the property, but the rest is treeless and is grazed by a few cattle and sheep. On the other side the pasture abuts the neighbouring acreage, one corner of which is bushland.

The people who own this block often hear their neighbours talk about seeing ringtailed possums in the trees, and are puzzled as to why they don't see any on their property. They learn that these beautiful possums are reluctant to come to the ground, preferring to go cross-country from tree to tree rather than risk coming to the ground. They also hear that ringtailed possum populations are declining. They work out that their largely treeless property is breaking up the flow of bushland in their area and decide to fence off and regenerate native bush in part of their block to create a wildlife corridor.

With some advice from Greening Australia and Bushcare the owners decide to sow seed directly into the soil on a half-acre block in early autumn, with follow-up sowing in spring if necessary. The seed is obtained from local native bushland, but they supplement the sowing by planting a few more advanced trees. The seedlings and the newly sown area are protected with a high wire fence with a floppy top, at least until the plants are established.

These landowners have begun their wildlife corridor with one animal species in mind. Yet when their plantings become established, they will no doubt be delighted by the variety of birds, insects and mammals that will use this wildlife corridor. They'll also be delighted by the flowers and foliage of their local plant species.

3. Growing your habitat garden

With the planning done, the simplest way to start growing your garden is to buy plants, ready for planting, from an indigenous nursery, local council or similar. However, not everyone wants to buy plants, because they either can't afford to or because they love the challenge and cost savings involved in do-it-yourself plant growing.

Propagation

Ever since Joseph Banks gave his name to specimens collected on Captain Cook's voyages, Australian plants have been taken and grown around the world. Well before that Australia's Aborigines knew a great deal about plant propagation, and manipulated the process through the use of carefully timed firing of patches of bushland.

Many home gardeners still know very little about how to propagate many of Australia's native plants, despite the fact that a great deal of research has gone into this subject in recent decades.

So why propagate?

Apart from being a fascinating and challenging activity, plant propagation can save you a lot of money. A habitat garden requires a great number of plants, and propagating your own will help to cut costs.

There are essentially two ways of propagating plants. You either plant a seed or you take a cutting. Following are the pros and cons for both methods.

Getting seed

Some standard nurseries and mail order firms stock native plant seeds. However

---

Growing plants from cuttings

A cutting is a piece taken from a growing plant, usually the shoot of a healthy stem. The butt of the stem is placed into a growing medium. The cutting 'takes' when the wound from the cut heals over and new roots develop. In many cases the use of a hormone rooting powder or liquid, and a free-draining growing medium such as coarse sand, will greatly increase the chances of success. Although there are many different types of cuttings, native plants generally tend to be propagated by soft tip or semi-hardwood cuttings. Follow the procedures outlined below.

- Take cuttings of flowering plants a month or two after they have finished flowering.
- Cut just below where a leaf joins the stem.
- Make cuttings about 10cm in length, and plant a third to half their length in the growing medium.
- Protect the planted cutting from sun and extremes of temperature.
- The use of a mini glasshouse, even a makeshift plastic roof over the pot, will help to keep temperature and humidity levels up.
- Beware of soil drying out (which kills the roots) or becoming too moist (which rots the roots).
- When new leaves appear start to harden the new plants by getting them gradually used to outside conditions.

Propagating from seeds

Pros:
- Well-stored seeds can be kept viable for long periods of time.
- Plants grown from seed are not genetically the same as the parent plant, so genetic diversity is enhanced.

Cons:
- Particular characteristics, say flower colour or plant shape, can't be guaranteed.
- Some plant seeds, for example, Boronias are very difficult to germinate, and others require special techniques, such as smoke exposure or heat treatment.

Propagating from cuttings

Pros:
- Being genetically the same as the parent plant so you know what you're getting.

Cons:
- Some plants will not 'take' from cuttings, or are difficult to handle.
- Can restrict the genetic diversity of plants which helps to keep plants ahead of disease and other threats.
- Must be used fresh, so supply must be ready and available.

for the habitat garden, where you're trying to grow local plants, you may be better off collecting your own seed, or getting it from a specialist local nursery or reputable organisation.

If you're going to gather your own seed, there are some basic rules that should be observed:

Make sure you have permission to get the seed. On public land this may require a permit. On private land it requires the consent of the landowner.

Collect seed from places which are near the garden you'll be planting in, or have similar site conditions

Try to collect each type of seed from a range of healthy plants that are spaced well apart. This will help to ensure genetic diversity.

Limit the amount of seed collected from any one plant so there's still plenty of seed for natural dispersal (10 per cent is a reasonable limit).

Germinating seeds

Not all seeds germinate easily, and this seems especially true of some Australian native plants. Many plants have adapted to the sometimes harsh and unpredictable nature of Australian conditions by chemically or physically inhibiting germination until conditions are right. With the right pre-treatment, it is often possible to mimic these conditions, although some genuses (including *Eremophila* and *Thryptomene*) continue to defy most efforts to propagate them from seed.

Some methods of seed treatment
Boiling water

The seeds of most *Acacias*, most members of the *Fabaceae* (pea flower family), and other species including *Senna*, respond well to the application of boiling water. This simulates the effects of bushfire and helps break down the hard coating of the seed, preparing it for germination. Simply place the seeds in a cup and pour boiling water over them. Leave overnight, and choose the seeds which have become swollen to sow into a growing medium. Seeds which haven't swollen up can either be treated again or discarded.

(continued page 22)

What, how and when to propagate: a table of selected plants

Plant	Propagation method	Best time
Acacia (wattles)	seed	Aug–Sept
Allocasuarina (she-oaks)	seed	Dec–Feb Mar–May
Angophora	seed	Sept–Nov
Anigozanthus (kangaroo paws)	division (virus-tested stock) seed (fresh)	Sept–Nov Sept–Nov
Araucaria	cuttings; seed	Dec–Feb
Asplenium	spores (2–3 weeks after ripening); division	Mar–May
Backhousia	seed	Sept–Nov
Baeckia	soft tip cuttings	Dec–April
Banksia	seed; soft tip cuttings	Sept–Nov
Bauera	soft tip cuttings; seed (8 weeks to germinate); layering	Sept–Oct
Billardiera	seed (difficult); division; soft tip cuttings	Mar–May
Blandfordia (Christmas bells)	seed	Sept–Nov
Boronia	soft tip cuttings	Sept–Nov
Brachychiton	seeds (wear gloves and mask as there are often hairs on seeds); graft onto seedling understock	Sept–Nov
Brachyscome (native daisies)	seed soft tip cuttings division	Sept–Nov Mar–May
Brachysema	seed soft tip cuttings	Sept–Nov Mar–Apr
Bracteantha (straw flowers)	seed; soft tip cuttings	
Callistemon (bottlebrushes)	seed from one-year-old woody fruits soft tip cuttings	Sept–Nov Dec–Jun
Callitris (cypress pines)	seed (viable for several years)	Mar–May
Calothamnus	seed (from one-year-old or older woody fruits) soft tip cuttings	Sept–Oct
Cassia (see also *Senna*)	seed soft tip cuttings	Sept–Nov Dec–Mar
Clematis	seed (fresh)	Sept
Correa	soft tip cuttings	Jan–Mar

What, how and when to propagate: a table of selected plants (cont.)

Plant	Propagation method	Best time
Crowea	soft tip cuttings	Jan–Mar
Cyathea	spores (2–3 weeks after ripening)	Mar–Apr
Dampiera	soft tip cuttings	Sept–Nov
Darwinia	seed; cuttings	Sept–Nov
Dendrobium	division	Mar–May
Dianella (native flax lilies)	division	Mar–May
Dicksonia	spores (2–3 weeks after ripening)	Mar–May
Dillwynia	seed; soft tip cuttings	Dec–Mar
Dodonaea	soft tip cuttings	Sept–Nov / Dec–Mar
Doryanthes (spear lilies)	seed (soak for several hours)	Sept–Nov
Drosera	division	Mar–May
	leaf cuttings	Sept–Nov
Dryandra	seeds	Sept–Nov
Epacris	seeds	Sept–Nov
	soft tip cuttings	Dec–Mar
Eremophila	soft tip cuttings	Sept–Nov
Eriostemon	soft tip cuttings	Mar–May
Eucalyptus (gum trees)	seed	Sept–Mar
Ficus	seed; fresh cuttings	
Gahnia (sword grass)	seed; division	Mar–May
Goodenia	seed; stem cuttings; stolons (runners or stems that take root)	Dec–Feb
Grevillea	soft tip cuttings	Dec–Feb
Hakea	seed (from sundried woody fruit)	Sept–Nov
	soft tip cuttings	Dec–Apr
Hardenbergia (false or native sarsaparilla)	seeds	Sept–Nov
	soft tip cuttings	Mar–Apr
Hibbertia (guinea flowers)	cuttings	summer
Hovea	seed	summer
Indigofera (indigo bush)	seed	Sept–Oct

What, how and when to propagate: a table of selected plants (cont.)

Plant	Propagation method	Best time
Isopogon (drumsticks)	seed; soft tip cuttings	Sept–Nov
Jasminum (native jasmine)	seed (pre-treatment)	
Kennedia (coral pea)	seed	Sept–Oct
	soft tip cuttings	Dec–Feb
Kunzea	soft tip cuttings	Feb–Apr
Lambertia	seed	Sept–Nov
	soft tip cuttings	Feb–Apr
Lechenaultia	soft tip cuttings	Sept–Nov
Leptospermum (tea trees)	seeds	Sept–Nov
	soft tip cuttings	May–Jun
Livistonia	seed	
Lomandra (mat rushes)	seed; division	Mar–May
Macadamia	seed (as soon as ripe – 6 months to germinate); graft	
Macrozamia	seed	
Melaleuca (paperbarks)	seed; soft tip cuttings	Sept–Nov
	soft wood cuttings	Dec–Mar
Melia	seeds (poisonous); soft tip cuttings	Sept–Nov
Myoporum (boobiallas)	soft tip cuttings	Sept–Mar
Nothofagus	seed	
Olearia (daisy bushes)	soft tip cuttings	
Pandorea	seed; soft tip cuttings	Sept–Mar
Pepperomia	leaf cuttings	
Persoonia	seed (difficult); soft tip cuttings	Sept–Mar
Phebalium	soft tip cuttings	
Pimelea (rice flowers)	soft tip cuttings	Nov–Dec
Pittosporum	seed	
Pomaderris	seed	
Prostanthera (native mint bushes)	soft tip cuttings	Nov–Dec
Pultaneae	seed; cuttings	Sept–Nov
Quandong	seed (moist, dark, stratification)	

What, how and when to propagate: a table of selected plants (cont.)

Plant	Propagation method	Best time
Scaevola (fan flowers)	soft tip cuttings	
Senna (see also *Cassia*)	seed	Sept–Nov
	soft tip cuttings	Dec–Mar
Sollya	seed; soft tip cuttings	Sept–Nov
Syzygium (lilly pillies)	soft tip cuttings	Dec–Mar
Telopea (waratahs)	seed	Jun–Jul
	soft tip cuttings	Sept
Thryptomene	soft tip cuttings	Sept–May
Verticordia (feather flowers)	soft tip cuttings	Sept–Nov
Viola (native violet)	division	all year
Westringia	soft tip cuttings	Mar–May
Xanthorrhoea	seeds	Sept–Nov
Zieria	soft tip cuttings	Dec–Mar

Table adapted from information kindly supplied by The Australian National Botanic Gardens (Education Unit), Canberra.

Abrasion

A similar effect to boiling water can be achieved by rubbing seeds between two sheets of sandpaper. Alternatively a tumbler or drink mixer can be lined with an abrasive paper and seeds can be shaken to break down the hard seed coating. *Acacia* and *Senna* are among the seeds that have been successfully treated in this way.

Dark storage

The ripe seed of some native grasses and Epacridaceae, including *Leucopogon* and *Epacris* can be stored in a dry, dark place for three to six months. This simulates dormancy in the soil without the risk of the seed rotting or being eaten. Be sure to label the container so you know what's in it and when it's due to come out.

Smoke and smoke water

Recent research has shown improved germination rates occur in some species when seeds are exposed to smoke or smoke water. Good results have been achieved with hard-to-germinate species such as *Calytrix*, *Pimelia*, *Eriostemon*, *Dianella*, *Lechenaultia*, *Hakea* and some *Grevilleas*. Applying smoke to seeds can be difficult for the home gardener. It involves lighting a smoking fire, using a mixture of dry and green native plant material in a large metal drum or similar. The smoke is funnelled over seed trays within a sealed plastic tent for at least one hour. Smoke-affected seed can then be sown.

Smoke water produces a similar effect without the need for a tent. The smoke is drawn out of the metal drum via a pipe

A compact layered planting with poa, dogwood, daisy bush and she-oak provides shelter, flowers, nest sites and insects.

A bird's eye view of an inner city area – not many habitat options here. Imagine what a few trees would add to this scene.

Semi-natural bushland merges into urban bush and backyards in Hobart, as it does in many of our towns and cities.

The booming call of the tawny frogmouth is often heard, though the bird itself may be harder to find. A superbly camouflaged forest hunter, it sits still in trees by day, hunting only at night. (Peter Tonelli)

Structural features such as logs, rocks and mulch add habitat niches to this planting.

Functional, beautiful and good habitat – a weeping tea tree covers an ugly brick wall.

Bursts of colour (Chrysocephalum and Wahlenbergia) through a newly mulched planting.

Similar species in a natural setting show what to aim for in a habitat garden.

Kangaroo grass (*Themeda australis*) – an attractive habitat grass which thrives right across Australia, including here near Alice Springs.

Different uses of grass. Seeding native grasses contrast with an introduced mown lawn. The native grass is richer in habitat terms and easier to maintain.

A thick layer of newspapers or old jute carpet underlay are both a good foundation for sheet mulching. Here a 10cm layer of hardwood mulch will be spread over the top.

Even corrugated iron can be used as a (temporary) sheet mulch to kill off grass before planting out the garden.

Hardwood chips (left) can be mixed with hardwood fines (right) to make a good all-purpose mulch.

Mulch and newly planted under-storey species contrast with established kangaroo grass (background).

The natural look to strive for. Here a flowering bottlebrush (*Callistemon pallidus*) blooms amid sagg and fallen logs.

Weeping grass (Ehrharta) is planted into newly laid mulch. Mulch is kept back from the stem to prevent disease.

Bird- and insect-attracting bottlebrushes, such as this lemon bottlebrush (*Callistemon pallidus*), are colourful, hardy and found in most parts of Australia. (*Ian Jeanneret*)

through a 20-litre container of water. Smoke is bubbled through the water for about an hour. The smoked water can then be frozen until required. If you don't want to bother making your own you can now buy proprietary forms of smoke water, such as 'Regen 2000' developed and sold by Kings Park and Botanic Garden in Perth, Western Australia. Alternatively contact your local branch of the Australian Plant Society.

To use smoke water soak seed in a 9:1 water:smoke water solution for about 12 hours. Remove from the solution and sow the seed in a growing medium and water as per normal sowings. If you've soaked more than you need, treated seed can be dried and re-used without further soaking.

A caution: Not all native plant seeds respond well to smoke water. Germination of some, including paper daisies (*Rhodanthe, Schoenia*), is actually inhibited by the application of smoke water. The seed of some other species can be damaged by the prolonged soaking in water. In short the process is new enough to require further experimentation, and something of a trial-and-error approach.

Cooling

The germination of some species, particularly those of alpine and semi-alpine origins, benefits from an enforced period of cold. The seed of species such as *Eucalyptus pauciflora, E. robertsonii, E. delegetensis, Banksia canei, B. saxicola*, and even some non-alpine species such as *Anigozanthos* (kangaroo paws) can be mixed into damp sand or vermiculite, wrapped in cling wrap, and stored in the body of your refrigerator for one to three months prior to sowing. This process simulates the cold dormant period experienced in alpine areas. Be sure to label the mixture so it doesn't end up spread on your toast!

The sowing and growing medium

While some growers use a different medium for sowing seeds and growing seedlings, it is possible to make do with the same mix for both. A mixture of 75-85 per cent washed river sand to 15-25 per cent peat moss or an equivalent absorbent material, such as coir peat has been used successfully for many years.

Planting the seed

Seeds can be sown into punnets, propagating trays, tubes, recycled pots or even old margarine tubs. While the choice is yours, I recommend sowing straight into tubes then thinning out, as this overcomes the need for pricking out or re-potting. Sow the seed into the moistened

> **Peat moss in the garden**
>
> Peat is an organic substance formed by the compression of dead plant material, such as various mosses, in the absence of oxygen. It is harvested, usually from bogland, and used in potting soil for its moisture retention qualities. The continuing use of peat is causing some environmental concerns, particularly to do with its long-term sustainability. Put simply, it is being harvested at a far greater rate than it is being formed. Fortunately it's now possible to use sustainable waste products, such as coir (coconut fibre) or composted pine bark, to achieve similar results. Ask your local nursery or garden supplier for details.

mixture and cover to a depth about twice the diameter of the seed. In the case of very fine seed you can either just press the seed into the mix, or else cover with a thin layer of very fine gravel or sand. Some other Dos and Don'ts:

- Don't sow your seed too thickly. This can increase the chance of fungal attack and may limit the space required for ideal seedling development.
- If watering your mix from overhead, use a gentle spray in order to avoid dislodging the seeds or damaging the seedlings.
- Keep the growing medium moist but not too wet as this may encourage the fungi that cause 'damping off'.
- Look out for pests such as slugs, snails or caterpillars, which can defoliate and kill your seedlings. Remove them by hand.
- If a fungus attacks a punnet or tray of seedlings, remove the whole tray and discard the potting mix. Only re-use the tray once it has been thoroughly washed and scrubbed clean in hot water.
- In cooler climates a heated propagation tray, or mini-glasshouse, may be beneficial. Certainly exposure to some sun and warmth is beneficial to the germination and growing process.
- Keep propagating boxes off the ground.
- Harden seedlings slowly by putting them in the shade and move them out into the sun for short periods, slowly increasing their time in the sun.

Getting growing

Germination times vary greatly from species to species. While *Acacias* may appear within a few days, especially when pre-treated, most plants will take a week or two to appear. Some, such as *Anigozanthos* (kangaroo paws), *Allocasuarinas* (she-oaks) and *Melaleuca* (paperbarks), take up to three weeks, while a few species can take months to germinate.

Once the seeds germinate and the seedlings are established in their tubes they should be gradually exposed to external weather conditions. To avoid the disruption of re-potting, seedlings can be planted out straight from their tubes. If they're to be kept for any length of time prior to planting, it's best to put seedlings into a larger container, for example, a 120mm or 150mm pot. They can then be planted out whenever you are ready.

Planting out

Whether you propagate your own seedlings or buy them from a nursery the same procedure for planting out should be followed.

Native plants and fertilisers

Australia's soils are generally starved of nutrients, and consequently much of our flora has developed without exposure to naturally occurring fertilisers. However it is NOT true that all native plants hate fertilisers. Most of our plants still require the nitrogen, phosphorous and potassium that are essential to plant growth. In certain cases Australian plants, including some *Acacias* and *Banksias*, can be harmed by exposure to phosphorous-rich fertilisers. The use of a controlled release fertiliser especially formulated for natives is often beneficial in the early stages of a seedling's life. Some of these fertilisers are now available in a low-phosphate or phosphate-free formulation.

Preparing the site Proper preparation of your site can ensure your habitat garden gets a flying start. This should be done according to the plan that you will already have drawn up in Chapter 2. When you are preparing the site, some of the following considerations need to be taken into account:

Weeds Is weed control necessary? Unless you are starting with a newly bulldozed block, you're likely to have weeds to deal with before you plant. Some gardeners choose to apply a broad spectrum herbicide such as Glyphosate to kill weeds. As this can have some residual environmental effects, an alternative is to sheet weed. One method of this is to thickly mulch with newspaper, at least 8–10 sheets thick, or jute carpet underlay followed by a thick layer of hardwood mulch (5–10cm thick). You can also use sheet weeding by putting slabs of corrugated iron or tin down to cover the grass and weeds. These sheets kill off the weeds by excluding light. Remove the sheets when the weeds are dead. Hand weeding or cultivation of anything but small sections of the garden is both time consuming and often futile. Cultivation is likely to bring up as many weeds as it removes.

Soil improvement New blocks are sometimes on hard clay or a similarly difficult base material. Often the block has been scraped clear of much of its surface soil and organic matter. In such a case the improvement of the soil, for example, the addition of gypsum to break up clay, or even the importing of soil may be considered. For a local habitat garden these improvements should mimic the soil that would once have covered the block. Once the soil has settled, planting can begin.

Earthworks To avoid tearing up your new plants, it's worth getting all earthworks such as sewerage, plumbing, power and roadworks, over and done with before you start planting. Conserve as much useful material as possible, such as soil or rock from any excavation work as you will be able to use this later in your new garden.

It is also worth considering any shaping or contouring of the land at this stage. With careful use of contouring it's possible to direct soil moisture and drainage into a pre-selected wetter area. This part of the garden can then be planted out with moisture-loving plants, like reeds and rushes, to create an ephemeral wetter habitat. This area could be linked in with a garden pond. Keep in mind that garden paths can also shed a great deal of water and the positioning is important in relation to the wet areas. Wherever possible consider how to direct water into appropriate parts of the garden before planting.

Existing plants Choose which, if any, of the plants already in your garden you want to keep. Try to keep as many local native plants as possible so there's some continuity for the living communities already relying on those plants. You may even keep some pre-existing non-native plants, at least on a temporary basis, so that not all cover is suddenly removed.

When to plant
It's best to avoid the extremes of either mid-winter or mid-summer. In much of

Australia the shortness of winter days and the possibility of frost can set back new plantings. Similarly the heat of summer can cause stress to young plants. As there are wide climatic variations across Australia, it's best to take note of local conditions. Generally autumn is the most benign season for planting as autumn days are still long enough and warm enough to promote initial growth without too much risk of heat stress. Where early frosts are a threat, you can protect seedlings by using plastic or material guards. If you can keep water up to your plants in the initial few months, then spring or early summer is a reasonable alternative.

What to plant Apart from the principles of *plant local species* and *layer your plants*, there are some other issues to think about when selecting suitable plants.

Plant mix It's tempting to put in the greatest variety possible in an effort to add 'spice' to your garden. Wherever it is feasible, local natural bushland should be your guide here. To get a clearer picture of what to put in the habitat garden, measure out and survey a 25m² (5m x 5m) section of local bushland, if possible. Make a note of the type of and number of species; get expert help with plant identification if you need to. You will generally find that the number of species found in a section of natural bush can be represented by a pyramid. The smaller species, such as groundcovers, herbs and grasses, will make up the largest number; medium-sized species, such as shrubs and smaller bushes, will be fewer in number; and larger species, such as trees and large bushes will be fewest of all.

Plant density It is also important to consider the density of plantings. On the principle that you are mimicking nature, this again will be partly determined by the density and variety of species found in your local natural bushland. This will alter according to site factors as rainfall, soil types, slope and aspect. Given a greater degree of control over some of these factors in the home garden, many gardeners choose to err on the side of putting in too many plants rather than too few. Generally speaking plant removal is a quicker and more effective way of achieving balance than filling in gaps. Another benefit is the potential to encourage habitat-enhancing creatures. For example, one *Lomandra* (mat rush) plant will attract a few butterflies and small mammals but a large clump of *Lomandra* will attract an even larger number of butterflies and mammals.

Plant size Finally, choose plants that suit your garden. Very large trees, for instance, have no place in the small suburban garden. They can be a potential threat to both people and buildings through falling over and/or losing large limbs during storms or strong winds. Always check the final size of the plant or ask your local nursery for advice.

Plants and fire Likewise in any fire-prone area, and that's potentially much of Australia, plants that are fire adapted or burn easily should not be grown close to a dwelling. These types of plants represent a potential danger to both people and buildings in the event of a bushfire. As well as favouring less flammable native plants, there are several other ways of

A selection of trees suitable for smaller gardens

This list contains species from many parts of Australia. In a habitat garden use only those species that occur naturally in your area.

Acacias including *Acacia aneura, A. cheelii, A. dunnii, A. fimbriata, A. papyrocarpa, A. perangusta, A. prominens.*

Allocasuarinas including *Allocasuarina distyla, A. inophloia, A. littoralis, A. verticillata.*

Banksias including *Banksia cunninghamii, B. dentata, B. marginata, B. menziesii, B. prionotes, B. serrata.*

Callitris including *Callitris monticola, C. oblonga, C. verrucosa.*

Eucalypts including *Eucalyptus caesia, E. crenulata, E. curtisii, E. diversifolia, E. forrestiana, E. macrandra, E. moorei, E. orbifolia, E. perriniana, E. spathulata, E. viridis.*

Some other smaller trees include Acronychia wilcoxiana, Agonis flexuosa, Angophora hispida, Callistemon viminalis, Hakea salicifolia, Hymenosporum flavum, Pittosporum rhomboidifolium, Tristaniopsis laurina.

reducing bushfire risk if you live in a fire-prone area. These include:
- Keeping a 'Fuel Modified Buffer Zone', that is, an outer zone which isolates the building from direct flame and radiant heat by keeping plant height and density down, and the use of less fire-prone plants. The width of this zone will vary, typically from 10m to 50m, depending on the slope and natural cover on your land.
- Having a 'Building Protection Zone', that is, an inner zone against the building where there is a minimum of fuel. The size of this zone will vary, typically from 15m to 40m depending on factors such as slope and natural cover. This inner zone can be created through the use of paving, vegetable or ornamental gardens, lawns, clothes drying areas, play areas and swimming pools. In the habitat garden these areas can also be used for potted bird- or insect-attracting plants.
- During the peak fire season you might consider raking mulch into rows or islands away from the Building Protection Zone, respreading it during the safer times. This way the mulch can still function as habitat throughout the year.
- Clearing your gutters of leaves, twigs and so on, especially before the fire season.
- Not storing firewood under the house.
- Storing flammable liquids away from the house.
- Keeping all access to your land as clear as possible.
- Having hoses strategically positioned in your garden.

How to plant

Pre-soak your plants by soaking potted seedlings in water for a couple of hours before planting. This will help establish them more quickly.

Make the planting hole slightly deeper than the pot and up to twice as wide.

Soak the planting hole, allow it to drain, then soak and drain again before

A selection of less fire-prone native plants

There is no such thing as a plant that doesn't burn. This list contains some plants which have been found to burn less easily under some conditions.

This list contains species from all around Australia. In a habitat garden, use only those species that occur naturally in your area.

Species Name	Common Name/s	Species Name	Common Name/s
Acacia species (including baileyana, dealbata, elata, howittii, melanoxylon, pravissima, prominens, saligna, vestita)	wattle	Eucalyptus species (including alpina, gummifera, lehmannii, and pauciflora)	gum tree
		Ficus macrophylla	Moreton Bay fig
Acmena smithii	lilly pilly	Hardenbergia violacea	false sarsaparilla
Agonis juniperina	native cedar	Kennedia prostrata (Also K. rubicunda)	running postman
Ajuga australis	austral bugle		
Banksia marginata	banksia	Lagunaria patersonii	Norfolk Island hibiscus
Brachychiton populneus	kurrajong	Melaleuca lanceolata	black tea tree
Bursaria spinosa	blackthorn	Myoporum insulare	boobialla
Carpobotrus glaucescens	pigface	Pittosporum species (including revolutum, rhombifolium, and undulatum)	pittosporum
Dichondra repens	kidney weed		

planting. This softens the surrounding soil, helping it to more readily take in the roots of the new plant.

If the potted plant has become root-bound, trim off the excess roots before removing from the pot.

Remove the plant from the pot by placing fingers over the soil in the pot and up-ending the pot into your hand. If necessary gently knock the base of the pot with a block of wood or similar, to dislodge the rootball.

Position Position the seedling in the hole so that it is slightly lower than the existing soil level. Backfill the hole with soil, pressing down to avoid air gaps.

Mulch Mulch to a depth of between 5cm and 10cm. Do not allow the mulch to come into direct contact with the stem of the seedling as this can encourage disease or fungal attack.

Water Water the plant well once. Only repeat as necessary, preferably with a long soaking rather than small bursts of watering.

Direct seeding of native plants for larger gardens

In very large gardens, or on rural properties or community projects where a mass planting of local native vegetation is required, it is worth considering direct

seeding. This method involves the sowing of seeds directly onto the land to be revegetated. It has several advantages, including:
- Seeds are much cheaper than seedlings, especially if you collect them;
- Plantings often have a more natural look;
- Time saving;
- Avoiding transplant shock;
- Healthier root systems.

Disadvantages can include the sometimes patchier initial results and the more complex preparation. This is especially true for the home gardener, who is unlikely to have access to the kinds of tools and materials that a rural holder has.

Preparing for direct seeding

Preparation begins with the removal of weeds and grass. This can be done by machine, with herbicide or by hand. Given the basic habitat garden principle that 'pests and weeds are managed naturally', chemical weeding is set aside. This leaves machine ploughing, which is unlikely to be done in the home garden, or mowing followed by sheet mulching. In the latter case, the mulch must be removed before seed sowing, and reapplied only when the plants have become reached a stage at which they require little or no watering to survive.

Seeds should include a selection of local species, from ground covers to shrubs to trees. For tips on collecting your own seeds see the 'Getting Seed' section on pp. 17–18. If you don't collect your own seeds, try to ensure that what you buy is from your local area. When trying to calculate how many seeds you will need, you should note that the survival/viability rate of seeds sown in this manner averages around 1 per cent, although this percentage increases in ideal conditions, such as a warm seedbed and follow-up rain. Even if you achieve a 5 per cent success rate you are going to need a lot of seeds. Some authorities recommend in excess of 1kg of seeds per hectare, depending on which species you are sowing.

Some seeds, particularly leguminous trees such as *Acacia*, will require treatment with boiling water before sowing. See the 'Some Methods of Seed Treatment' section on pp. 18, 22–23.

Seeds will take better if the soil is worked to create a seedbed, and the seeds are covered after sowing. This can be achieved by a light raking over the soil or by dragging a hessian bag over the area. Be aware that the seedbed will also be ideal for weeds, which may spring up to out-compete the native plants. Weeding at least twice in the weeks after the seedlings sprout will be necessary until the seedlings are big enough to out-compete most weeds. It is also be important to initially exclude stock, native animals and vermin from the area. This can be achieved by using a floppy fence made with a rabbit-proof lower section. See the 'Protecting your vegetable, fruit and flower gardens' section on pp. 56–57.

Plantings around eucalypts

Planting new shrubs beneath established eucalypts (gum trees) can present a number of problems. Firstly eucalypts and some other trees protect themselves from competition by using their own form of chemical warfare. In what is called an

A selection of shade-tolerant native plants

This list contains species from all around Australia. In a habitat garden use only those species that occur naturally in your area. Inclusion in this list does not imply that these plants will necessarily thrive beneath eucalypts or any other established trees.

Species Name	Common Name/s
Acacia species (including *brownii*, *drummondii*, *riceana* and *schinoides*)	wattle
Archontophoenix alexandrae	Alexander palm
A. cunninghamiana	Bangalow palm
Artanema fimbiatum	
Astroloma – some species	
Asperula species	
Austromyrtus species	
Baeckea species, including *Baeckea densifolia* and *linifolia*	
Bauera rubioides	Bauera, river rose, dog rose
Blechnum species	water ferns
Boronia – most species	Boronia
Brachyscome aculeata	Brachyscome, native daisy
Bulbine bulbosa	rock lily
Callicoma serratifolia	blackwattle
Calytrix alpestris	Calytrix, fringe myrtle
Commelina cyanea	native wandering jew
Cordyline species	Cordyline
Correa species, including *aemula*, *bauerlenii*, *glabra*, *pulchella* and *schlechtendalii*	Correa, native fuchsia
Crowea – most species	Crowea
Cyathea species	tree fern
Darwinia species, including *citriodora*, *fascicularis* and *procera*	
Daviesia species	
Derwentia derwentiana, and *D. perfoliata*	Derwentia
Dianella species	flax lily
Epacris species	heath
Flindersia (most species)	leopard tree, Australian teak, crow's ash
Goodenia (some species including *hederacea*, *heterophylla* and *pinnatifida*)	Goodenia
Grevillea species (including *acanthifolia*, *aquifolium*, *australis*, *barklyana*, *longifolia* and *willisii*)	Grevillea
Hibbertia (some species, including *cuneiformis*, *diffusa*, *obtusifolia* and *stellaris*)	guinea flowers
Hovea species	Hovea
Hybanthus monopetalus	
Hydrocotyle peduncularis	
Leptospermum species (including *arachnoides*, *brachyandrum*, *epacridoideum*, *lanigerum*, *macrocarpum*, *minutifolium*, *nitidum*, *obervatum* and *scoparium*)	tea tree
Lomandra (some species including *banksii*, *hystrix*, *longifolia* and *obliqua*)	Lomandra, Sagg

A selection of shade tolerant native plants (cont.)

Species Name	Common Name/s
Lomatia species	Lomatia
Macrozamia (most species)	Burrawang
Melaleuca species (including *alternifolia, densa, ericifolia, groveana* and *hypericifolia*)	paperbark
Nestegis ligustrina	
Olearia species (including *argophylla, elliptica, iodochroa, megalophylla, stellulata* and *viscosa*)	daisy bush
Phebalium species	
Pittosporum species (including *bicolor, o'reillyanum, revolutum* and *rubiginosum*)	Pittosporum
Podolepis species (including *monticola* and *robusta*)	
Prostanthera species (including *lasianthos* and *prunelloides*)	Christmas bush, mint bush
Pultenaea species (including *daphnoides, flexilis, gunnii* and *stipularis*)	bacon and eggs
Tasmannia species (including *insipida, lanceolata, purpurascens, stipitata* and *xerophila*)	pepper bush
Tetratheca (most species)	black-eyed Susan
Phyla nodiflora	
Scutellaria humilis	dwarf skullcap
Viola hederacea	native violet
Zieria arborescens	

allelopathic response, the specific plants release chemicals into the surrounding environment which inhibit the growth of shrubs and seedlings of other trees, even including their own seedlings. However, not all plants are put off by this un-neighbourly behaviour.

This gives you a couple of options when planting near eucalypts. Either choose species which are not susceptible to the effect of gum tree chemistry, or plant outside the range of the toxins.

For the first option, observe which plants survive under eucalypts in your area, or else ask a local native plant nursery for advice. Plants such as, *Banksia, Grevillea, Lomandra, Xanthorroea, Westringia, Poa* and *Scaevola*, plus some ferns and some *Acacias* are among the many which seem to co-exist happily with mature eucalypts.

The other option is to plant a distance away that's equal to at least twice the height of the mature tree.

If you're planting out eucalyptus seedlings, there is usually no problem planting other species nearby. By the time the tree is large enough to effect those plants they will either be established enough to resist or, in the case of shrubs, they'll be near the end of their life cycle anyway.

Some other issues to keep an eye out for when planting beneath established trees of any sort are water stress and shade.

Water stress

Established native trees, especially eucalypts, tend to hog water. Any seedlings you plant out beneath them will need extra care in terms of watering, either by hand or through some sort of irrigation system. If you hand water it helps to place a piece of irrigation or drainage pipe (the sort with holes in it) into the planting hole, with the top of the pipe sitting just above the surface and the bottom at or around root level. Pouring water into the top of the pipe delivers it directly to the roots, where it is most necessary. Surface watering may result in saturation of only the top few centimetres of soil and subsequent water stress for the seedling.

Beware of trying to build up garden beds for your new plantings beneath gum trees. Even established eucalypts can be damaged if their surface roots are buried too deep.

Shade

The best way to combat shade is to choose plants that can cope with it to some degree. Again you can discover this by seeing what grows well in the shade in any of your local bushland. Or you can ask at a plant nursery, making sure to point out that you want *local* shade-loving species. The list on pp. 30–31 contains some suggestions.

4. Maintaining your habitat garden

Water and habitat gardening

Water is essential in the habitat garden. There are some different and particular approaches that the habitat gardener needs to take when it comes to water in this type of garden. For a start, water isn't just for plants. In the habitat garden it also provides for thirsty animals and is the medium in which many other animals live, breed and feed.

Australia is generally very dry, with nearly three-quarters of the continent receiving less than 500mm of annual rainfall. While most of us live in the better watered parts of the country, dry spells and drought are still a factor. So where many gardeners might be tempted to drought-proof their garden with elaborate and expensive watering systems, the habitat gardener will hesitate. Our native plants and animals have adapted to these dry conditions over a very long period of time. By favouring local species, habitat gardeners are adapting their garden to the climate rather than trying to create a different climate for their garden. Keep in mind Principle 3 and watch your water in the garden. The benefits are both short- and long-term.

Waterwise habitat gardening

Know your site

Very few single gardens have uniform soils, uniform aspects and uniform water requirements. There are usually shady spots, damp sections, dry areas and rocky or hilly spots. These areas will suit different plants and animals, and will require different approaches when it comes to water. Diversity is what you want in a habitat garden, so plan your water use around these differing needs. For instance, putting your garden pond in an existing damp spot will not only limit the amount of additional water required, it will also more likely suit the species used in ponds – ones that are already adapted to the wet.

Plant selection

Choosing plants that suit your particular garden, AND the subtly different zones within your garden, you'll be able to limit the amount of artificial watering required. Local plants that are adapted to matching areas in your garden are generally going to require less of your attention. In my own garden a damp, shady gully has been planted out in plants that thrive in the damp, such as tree ferns, dogwood and musk. In a drier spot, choose plants with low water requirements. The grouping of plants according to their water requirements will make your watering more efficient. Look in your local bushland or ask local plant groups or nurseries for advice.

Mulching

Mulching has many benefits for the habitat gardener, particularly the prevention of water loss through evaporation. Mulches come in two broad categories, organic and artificial. Artificial mulches include plastic sheets and other synthetic materials such as nylon and acrylic carpet and synthetic underlay. Proprietary weed mats are also now available at garden suppliers. They have their place, and are certainly good at suppressing weed growth, but they will not break down and contribute organic matter to the soil. While this increases their lifespan, it decreases their contribution to natural cycles.

Organic mulches come in a bewildering variety. For the habitat gardener the best materials are ones that mimic the natural plant matter in your local area. If you live in an area with plenty of eucalypt bark and leaf matter, then using gum bark and leaves will be far better for local species than using pine chips or straw. Don't gather mulching material from your local bushland. This will only impoverish that area in favour of yours, with no nett benefit to the local environment. Buy in mulching material from gardening professionals, preferably ones that harvest it from your local area. While council tree loppers often mulch as they go, and supply it to home gardeners at a very reasonable cost, beware of the possibility of seeds from weed species, such as cotoneaster or privet, being delivered with the mulch. Mulch from land clearing or forestry may be an alternative in some areas.

Lawn alternatives

Conventional grass lawns require a great deal of input from the gardener. They are especially demanding in their use of water, largely because lawn grass species usually come from countries with abundant rainfall. The classic bowling green lawn may be suitable to parts of Europe, but in most of Australia it requires the skills and time of a greenkeeper to maintain one. Even though some newer grass varieties mean it's possible to have a lawn in Australia AND minimise water use, for the habitat gardener the alternatives to lawns are far more attractive. By minimising or eliminating lawn you will save water. And you will encourage not only plant species diversity, but also a new range of habitat niches for animal species that are not adapted to lawns, which includes most of our local species.

Watering systems

While there are many ways to water a garden, the habitat gardener needs to ask themself an important question: 'Am I going to put any extra water into my garden at all?' This question comes from the broader issue of how much the habitat gardener chooses to intervene in the garden. Some gardeners may choose not to water at all and simply 'let nature take its course'.

Most gardeners, however, are willing to intervene enough to at least see their plants established. Drip watering systems, which can distribute water to very specific areas, are a good compromise here.

Mulching

Mulch is a generic word for virtually any material that is spread over the surface of the soil to protect and help the plants growing there. One person's rubbish is another person's mulch, and a huge variety of materials have been used as

Lawn alternatives

Why mow and water your life away when there are so many other uses the habitat gardener can put a lawn to? Here are just a few.

Native grasses
Plant native grassland instead of lawn. Use species such as *Poa*, Kangaroo grass *(Themeda* species), Wallaby grass *(Chionchloa* species) or other native grasses that suit your area. These grasses require an occasional trim, usually after seeding, rather than mowing; they need much less water and will attract insects, birds and other native animals.

Mulching and planting out
Sheet mulch the lawn and plant out with local native shrubs, bushes and trees. If you use colourful flowering species, this will become a far more interesting feature than lawn.

Paving and pots
In areas where low growth is important (such as near the clothesline or barbecue area) you can pave the lawn area with flagstones or pavers, and have your plants restricted to pots. Many native species will thrive in a pot, and still attract birds and insects.

Wildflower meadows
Develop border areas around existing lawn that allow taller native grasses and wildflowers to encroach on the lawn, rather like the 'rough' of a golf course. These areas will attract birds and insects, and will reduce the amount of lawn that needs mowing and watering.

Groundcovers
Experiment with native groundcover plants that suit your area. Some widely applicable species include *Dichondra, Scaevola, Scleranthus, Kennedia* and prostrate forms of *Grevillea* (for example, *G. repens* and *G. 'Poorinda Royal Mantle'*).

Features.
Develop a water garden, a rockery or similar habitat feature where your lawn used to be.

---

mulch, most commonly straw, bark and leaf litter, wood chips, newspaper, gravel, plastic sheeting, even carpet underlay.

Why mulch?
Mulch is one of the great multipurpose garden helpers. It suppresses weed growth, retains moisture in the soil, moderates soil temperature and prevents erosion. It can also become a habitat in its own right, providing refuge for invertebrates which, in turn, supply food for birds, mammals and reptiles.

Eventually any organic mulch also breaks down as a soil-improving material, providing a suitable bed for seeds from your plants.

How much mulch?
Since you're mimicking a local habitat, be guided by the extent of mulch found in your local bush. As you're also trying to favour the local species over weeds and other exotic species, you may choose to start with a mulch that is both thicker and more widespread than occurs in nature.

This will limit the regrowth of the plants you don't want and make your weeding job easier. In most areas a mulch that is about 10–15cm deep will be plenty. Keep in mind that organic mulch is never a permanent fixture in the garden. Depending on what you use, the mulch will break down over a period of months or years. By that time your plants will hopefully be more established, and you can choose to be less liberal with the next lot of mulch. If you don't want to use mulch over the whole garden, you can choose to mulch around selected plants or else mulch for short periods.

Mulch and new planting

Freshly chipped mulch and newly planted seedlings do not go well together. New mulch, even local hardwood mulch, should be left for at least a few weeks before being spread around new seedlings. Otherwise there is a risk that the mulch could burn or even kill sensitive seedlings. Turning over and watering the mulch pile prior to spreading it will speed up the process of breaking down some of the more volatile substances, such as tannins.

It is also a good idea to keep mulch back from the collar of new plants. An alternative mulch, such as carpet underlay, about a square foot or so around each plant can be used.

Mulch, such as this fresh hardwood mulch, needs to sit for a while before being spread in order to minimise its potential toxic effect on plants.

What do I mulch with?

What you use as a mulch depends on where you live and what is available in your area. In a habitat garden it is generally best to use materials that mimic those found in your local bush. Often this will be hard-leaved native plant materials such as leaves, sticks and bark from hardwoods. Hardwood chips mixed with fine materials can mimic bush materials quite well. In areas where weed suppression is a major concern you can combine hardwood mulch with some other form of blanketing material. Try thick layers of newspaper or organic carpet underlay as a bottom layer with a thick layer of mulch on top.

Non-native plant materials, such as pine bark or pine chips, should not be used in the habitat garden. Pine leaches acid into the soil as it breaks down, and can burn native plants or suppress their growth. Inorganic mulch such as plastic sheeting or synthetic underlay will suppress weed growth well enough, but these materials can also prevent the penetration of water. Synthetics will disrupt the environment of soil-dwelling animals, and will never break down to provide a tilth in which native plants can self-seed.

Bush rocks in the habitat garden

Bush rocks – rocks that are partly or wholly exposed above ground level – are valued in any garden for their natural look. The growth of lichens or mosses on the surface enhances that appeal. Bush rocks also play a valuable role in the natural environment. Rocks can:

- provide shelter and a heat source for animals;
- provide a mulching effect;
- provide a place of germination for windborne seeds and help with rapid re-establishment of plant and animal communities following bushfires;
- protect soil from the effects of drying and erosion;
- act as a thermo-regulating barrier during weather changes;
- act as a fire retardant by reducing fuel.

Rocks are also, ultimately, the major source of the soil that sustains so much of life. Removing bush rocks from their natural habitat for use in your habitat garden is a case of 'robbing Peter to pay Paul'. It is also illegal in most areas unless you have a permit to do so.

So what are the alternative sources of rocks or similar materials that will enable you to leave bushland habitats unharmed while enhancing your habitat garden? If your land already has bush rocks, you are free to use them, preferably in or close to their original setting. If your block is being cleared before building or landscaping, ask to have any rocks set aside for later landscaping.

Alternatives to bush rock include:
- quarried rubble;
- stone flagging;
- sawn stone;
- mulch (with wire on slopes);
- railway sleepers;
- log timber lengths;
- bricks;
- subtle use of cement;
- artificial rocks.

The issue of aesthetics, how good the alternatives will look, can be helped by giving these materials an 'aged' look with the application of natural materials. Eucalyptus bark or leaves will stain when left on wet surfaces. Ochre, mud, well-rotted manure or compost can also be rubbed into rocks. The growth of lichen and other microscopic organisms can be encouraged by wetting your bush stone and applying a mixture of water and milk or yoghurt.

Pruning native plants

Should you prune plants in the habitat garden at all? Given that you are striving for the natural look, you may decide to leave them completely alone. On the other hand even the most naturalistic garden is likely to require the odd trim. Paths, for instance, need to be kept clear of plants. The shape, lifespan and flowering time of a plant can be helped by careful pruning.

The question then becomes, how do you prune native plants? There is no single answer, as some plants respond well to heavy pruning, while others can be devastated by a light trim. At the risk of generalising, it's fair to say that most bushes and shrubby plants can be trimmed lightly during their early growing years. It's also true that the pruning of mature plants is more likely to present problems.

Many native plants, including banksias, eucalypts and paperbarks, have lignotubers (swellings between the roots and the base of the trunk) from which they can regenerate after fire. Heavy pruning of these types of plants, even cutting them off at ground level, will often cause a similar reaction, with fresh shoots coming from the lignotubers at ground level. A more cautious approach is generally recommended. If in doubt when pruning native bushes and shrubs, it is best to:
- prune back plants that are still developing;
- prune back no more than 30 per cent;
- cut only green and growing parts;
- be sure that there is plenty of green foliage remaining.

When it comes to pruning trees, the same general guidelines apply. However it is even more important to focus on the early years of a tree's growth. This gives you some control over the general shape it will develop. It is also far easier to reach a sapling's branches than those of a mature tree. Serious pruning of mature trees should be left to a professional tree surgeon.

The pruning of grasses, groundcovers and clumping plants will be a more individual matter. You may choose to mimic the grazing effect of native animals, or leave the plants untouched – perhaps waiting until the grazers come into your garden. If you choose to prune, groundcovers such as correas and hibbertias respond to pruning in much the same way as larger shrubs and bushes. Grasses such as poas, weeping grasses and wallaby grasses respond well to a 50 per cent 'haircut' shortly after seeding but they do not like to be mown flat in the way that most introduced lawn grasses do.

Managing weeds and pests

A habitat gardener aims toward a system that is in natural balance. Even the best of habitat gardens is just part of a larger system, and that larger system is all too often out of balance. It is alarmingly easy to find instances of unbalanced habitats, even in rural and bushland areas. Dieback of eucalypts is a widespread example. All over rural Australia, as a result of tree removal, over-grazing, and insect and animal attack, gum trees are dying and are not being replaced.

In a balanced system for instance, the population of leaf-eating beetle larvae will be kept down by the birds and other insects that prey on them. If the number of trees that the larvae feed on are reduced and the number of the larvae's predators are, in turn, reduced, the possibility of plague numbers occurring is increased. Plagues result in severe or even fatal damage being done to the remaining trees, a habitat imbalance that leads to disaster.

A habitat that is in balance is less likely to be troubled by pest attacks. In the process of achieving such a balance, and even once a garden is in balance, there are still issues of pest management. That's because such a balance is dynamic, with weeds and animal pests being an ever present factor, even in the best of habitats.

In this natural bushland, rocks play an important role in varying the available habitat niches as well as altering the microclimate. (*Ian Jeanneret*)

Learning seed collecting at an early age, these young students are taking part in a school-based indigenous planting program in Canberra. It's important not to take too much of the viable seed; 10 per cent is a wise guideline. (*Mark Butz*)

Learning by doing. A volunteer parent helps a student plant out a seedling in a school-based indigenous planting program in Canberra. (*Mark Butz*)

Care and patience have their rewards. Here a community planting in Canberra is shown over a period of three years. At first the planting looks nothing much, but after just three years it has thickened into an impressive woodland. (*Mark Butz*)

Scleranthus biflorus makes a fine spreading groundcover, especially around rocks.

Flowering gums such as this Tasmanian blue gum (*E. globulus*) attract invertebrates, birds and mammals in massive numbers. In the case of the blue gum that includes the vulnerable swift parrot. (*Ian Jeanneret*)

Running postman (*Kennedia prostrata*) is not only an attractive groundcover but also a fire-resistant species.

Bird- and insect-attracting plants, including billy buttons (*Craspedia*) and sagg (*Lomandra longifolia*), can flower in the shade of eucalypts (here a yellow box, *E. melliodora*).

The beautifully coloured Swift Parrot has been declared a vulnerable species. It depends on blue gums (*E. globulus*) for its food and nest sites during the breeding season. (*Peter Tonelli*)

Currawongs – in this case a Tasmanian Black Currawong – are very curious birds, and will often visit a disturbed site (such as a newly mulched garden) to see what's on offer. They can be extremely aggressive towards other birds, although a healthy layered habitat should provide room and shelter for all local birds. (*Peter Tonelli*)

A juvenile Brown Goshawk. These birds inhabit wooded areas throughout Australia. (*Peter Tonelli*)

Grey or White Goshawks are a jewel to be found in forested areas from northern to southeastern Australia, including Tasmania. (*Peter Tonelli*)

Brown Falcons are found throughout Australia, hunting small mammals and birds virtually anywhere except in closed forest. (*Peter Tonelli*)

The Collared Sparrowhawk can be seen in the skies above most parts of the country. (*Peter Tonelli*)

The ultimate visitor to a wetland garden with a large pond or dam, the Black Swan requires large amounts of aquatic vegetation as food. (*Peter Tonelli*)

Eucalypts in bloom attract invertebrates, birds and small mammals.

This flowering grevillea provides insect- and bird-attracting flowers as well as dense foliage suitable for sheltering small birds.

So what do you do about managing pests if they become a major problem in your habitat garden?

For many years gardeners used chemical 'bombs' to combat pests. These 'bombs' were usually herbicides or insecticides which were sprayed on the 'enemy' species. But as in any war, the innocent died alongside the guilty. We now know that some pesticides, most notoriously DDT, have had devastating and wide-ranging effects on the global environment. Even with so-called safe sprays you are likely to kill non-target as well as target species.

Integrated pest management

In agriculture the term 'integrated pest management' has arisen in the last 20 years as a way of describing a more environmentally friendly way of managing pests. Integrated pest management looks at all possible methods of controlling pests, with the use of chemicals as a last resort. There are generally considered to be four major control methods. These are:

Cultural control

Know the enemy. Know its 'culture', what it likes and dislikes, and make the environment less attractive to it. For example, many fungi harmful to seedlings thrive on moisture and close contact with the host plant. Leaving the area immediately around a new seedling clear of mulch and other materials can deter fungal infection. Watering early in the day can also help to keep moisture around the trunk to a minimum, discouraging the conditions in which fungi thrive.

If making the environment less attractive for some species is the negative side of cultural control, keeping your garden attractive to beneficial species is the positive. Blue-tongue lizards are a beneficial species because they keep snails and slugs under control. Providing habitat features for them will be to your advantage.

Physical control

If you've ever pulled out a weed, excluded a rat, pruned a dead branch or trapped a wasp, you've used physical control. In fact, this is probably the most common form of pest control, though it may also be the most time-consuming. Some physical pest control methods can save a lot of hard work in the long run. Mulching is one example as it suppresses weed growth and promotes healthy soil conditions for the plants you want to thrive. Mulching can save you plenty of weeding and maintenance later.

Biological control

Properly used, biological control comes closest to being the 'smart bomb' for

---

The home gardener and chemical sprays

While researchers continue to look for chemicals which are less toxic to birds and mammals but still effective against targeted pests, gardeners are right to remain wary of chemical pest control. Chemical control is rarely needed in the urban garden. This is doubly true in the habitat garden which, after all, is mimicking the bush. How often do you see a major pest outbreak in healthy native bushland? The safest approach is to tolerate damage and resist the use of chemicals wherever possible.

gardeners. This form of control became famous in Australia when the introduced prickly pear cactus was all but eradicated by the introduction of a moth larva which fed specifically on the cactus. Other more recent biological control methods include the use of bacteria to control mosquito larvae and caterpillar larvae. An advantage of biological control is that it can be specific to a particular pest and won't affect non-target species. Biological control tends to be mainly used on commercial crops and vegetables but there are occasions for its use in the habitat garden.

Chemical control
Because of lessons learned from our indiscriminate use of chemicals in earlier decades, many gardeners are unwilling to use chemical control at all. Chemicals are particularly harmful to birds and other animals at the top of the food chain, and have been implicated in the demise of birds in woodland next to agricultural areas.

Some gardeners still see the careful and sparing use of chemicals as one possibility or as a method of last resort. And it is true that not all chemicals are as bad as one another. For example, substances including hormones and pheromones can successfully target pests like cockroaches and fleas, preventing them from maturing and reproducing.

So integrated pest management involves looking at all of these potential control methods. Integrated pest management also involves knowing precisely what is in your garden, so that one method of control doesn't inadvertently harm other species that you weren't aware of. Many gardeners might need to rely on the knowledge and expertise of others when it comes to pest management. That's fine, though it may be wise to exercise discretion when it comes to using some methods recommended by some gardeners. Not everyone will be as cautious as most habitat gardeners when it comes to the use of chemicals. If in doubt, seek advice from people such as Greening Australia, your local council or state environment department. And remember that a habitat in balance is the best form of pest management.

Tolerance of damage
One ideal of the habitat gardener in relation to pests is to develop a certain tolerance of plant damage. Two things come into play here. First, tolerating a certain amount of leaf loss to insects will mean you are slower in reaching for chemical solutions. Second, an acceptance of a certain amount of damage, and the possibility of a short-term 'messy' look, can end up creating a healthier ecosystem. When a tree falls in the forest, every living thing in the forest hears it. And before long the formerly vertical life form becomes a horizontal larder for a host of creatures. While you may not leave a fallen tree in your backyard, the principle is the same. Natural damage done to one part of an ecosystem generally creates opportunities for others.

When is a plant a weed?
To put it simply, a weed is any plant growing where we don't want it to grow. For a crop farmer that may mean native wattles sprouting in the middle of an introduced crop, for a greenkeeper it might mean native grasses appearing in a putting green.

For the habitat gardener whose focus is on favouring local species, the major concern is the presence of introduced species. That doesn't only mean plants introduced from overseas. Not every native plant is welcome in every habitat. For example, in much of New South Wales the Cootamundra wattle (*Acacia baileyana*) is a highly sought after native plant, its glorious flowers signalling the turn of the seasons towards spring. However, in other states Cootamundra wattle is considered a weed. It often escapes from gardens and invades native bush, where it out-competes local species and alters whole habitats. That said, it is still usually exotic plant species, especially noxious weeds, that are of most concern to the habitat gardener.

What is a noxious weed?

Weeds are called noxious if they pose a threat to the environment, to humans or to agriculture. Most states have a noxious plant list, and any weed found on such a list must be either controlled or removed. As every gardener knows, this is easier said than done. In the case of any sort of serious infestation of plants like blackberry, gorse, or broom, it is best to seek the advice of your local council or similar authority.

Threats to the habitat garden

Cats: a major threat to the habitat garden

The domestic cat poses one of the greatest threats to the habitat garden, as it does to the wider environment. Surveys have shown that the average domestic cat kills about 100 birds, not to mention other animals, every year of its life. Most of the birds killed are native birds, which haven't evolved alongside these talented killers and haven't developed defence strategies as many introduced birds have. If you multiply that death toll by the total number of domestic and feral cats throughout Australia, the figure becomes truly frightening.

Despite the considerable ecological cost of keeping cats, Australians seem unlikely to give them up. Cats can be wonderful companions and there are ways in which we can limit the damage they do. In some local government areas there are cat curfews, and cat catchers can impound any feline found prowling after dark, just as dogs have been treated for years.

What you can do

Put your cat under a curfew. This will certainly reduce the toll on wildlife, even if it doesn't stop your cat killing during the day.

Put bells and/or reflectors on your cat. Again this will help, although studies have shown that a hunting cat can prevent a bell from ringing until it springs. Then it's often too late for the prey to escape.

Desex your cat. This will stop it from roaming as much, reducing the amount of opportunistic hunting it engages in.

Keep your cat in an enclosure. This is a completely enclosed cat yard, containing everything your cat needs. One way to do this is to enclose the underside of a deck. The cat can use that space, and be given access to the inside of the house via a ramp and flap.

Short of not having cats at all, the key to minimising their impact is thoughtful and responsible cat ownership, taking some or all of the measures outlined above.

Is this cat friendly or feral? Our wildlife can't stop to ask because the damage done is often the same. (*Ingrid Albion*)

The snail menace – and how to beat it

Snails and slugs are a notorious threat to the vegetable or ornamental garden. But they can also munch their way through seedlings and even some established plants in the habitat garden. There are various ways of combating these pests, some of them are environmentally friendly, some less so.

Chemical control

There are three main snail control chemicals commonly available in Australia. They are usually green, bran-coloured or blue. The green pellets use *metaldehyde*, an effective poison which has a couple of disadvantages. First, it can kill earthworms and other soil organisms. Second, it tends to break down quickly in wetter weather. These problems can be avoided by placing the baits in containers that keep them out of contact with the soil and the weather.

Bran-coloured snail pellets contain *complexone*, an iron-based chemical, and are the least toxic of the commercial snail baits. These pellets are unlikely to harm domestic or native animals unless used in very large quantities. They also break down harmlessly in the soil.

The blue pellets contain *methiocarb* or *mesurol*. Although quite effective against slugs and snails, these chemicals can also kill non-target species. This means it affects not only cats and dogs, but also local habitat species. Secondary poisoning where animals are affected by eating poisoned snails, can be avoided by collecting dead snails and slugs immediately.

42 Habitat Garden

Non-chemical methods

One animal likely to be as keen as you are on catching snails and slugs is the blue-tongue lizard. If you can encourage them into your habitat garden you will both be happy – you because of their delightful presence and their snail-devouring abilities; the blue-tongue because of the food, shelter and safety you offer them. (See pp. 69–71 in Chapter 5 for hints on the best ways to care for blue-tongues in your garden.)

You can also take an active role in controlling snails and slugs. You can hunt them out by looking in such hiding places as against sheltered walls, in the foliage of favoured plants and around drains or damp spots. You can also wait for a rainy night and go collecting while the snails are out eating and socialising.

Some other ways of dealing with snails and slugs include setting and regularly checking traps, such as upturned pots, propped up to allow entry, or a half-buried bowl containing some beer. Snails and slugs are attracted to the yeasty smell, go in for a drink then drown, hopefully without feeling a thing. Whatever you choose to do about snails and slugs, there is no magic bullet that will eradicate them forever.

Changing with your habitat garden

Maintaining a habitat garden isn't a matter of keeping it looking the same year after year. If a garden is a work of art, it is one that is never finished. Unlike a painting or a sculpture, a garden is always having pieces added to or subtracted from it. Plants die or fail to thrive, or thrive so well that they have to be cut back. Experiments fail or new and possibly better ideas need to be tried.

The natural habitat is constantly changing, so too is a habitat garden. When your habitat garden is first started, it is immature. That doesn't make it inferior as habitat, just different. New plants won't immediately provide the foliage, flowers, fruit or nesting sites that mature plants do. It also takes time for 'word to spread' to the birds and mammals that your garden is friendly to local species. For example, a tiny eucalypt sapling won't make a suitable lookout for a frogmouth. But will be fine for spiders, insects or the smaller animals that live on them.

As the garden matures, ecological niches, the spaces that are occupied and used by plants and animals, will change and develop. Some of these changes will be through your decisions and hard work. But much of the change is due to the dynamics and the impermanent character of natural habitats.

Consider the life story of a short-lived tree, the silver wattle (*Acacia dealbata*). It is a prolific and fast growing sapling. It flowers when young and is soon attracting birds and insects with both food and shelter. But the wattle also attracts borers, the larvae of moths and beetles, which weaken the wattle's brittle limbs and eat into its heartwood. Within a few years it is tall but is already prone to losing limbs. This creates gaps that birds, such as parrots choose for nesting holes.

As the tree matures it grows taller, providing more space for birds, mammals, insects and fungi. Humans even put a swing or rope ladder onto its limbs, and children climb onto the stouter parts of the tree. But the dry years, wet years and insect attack take their toll. One winter a strong windstorm uproots the tree.

The loss of the tree saddens the gardener but in the natural economy nothing is really lost. The silver wattle's death is part of the continuation of life cycles. It has been host to dozens of species. In its death it still contributes as mulch or soil or in numerous other ways. And the space that it no longer occupies will become the place in which new life can thrive. All of this may occur in less than 20 years with the space in and around the tree constantly changing, the ecological niches coming and going.

Other plants will have shorter or longer timetables but the point is the same. A habitat garden is a dynamic place. Don't think of it only in terms of a grand master plan, a perfectly laid-out and finished masterpiece. Forget the television backyard makeover programs, where a total garden is created in one frantic weekend of effort. If you want a habitat garden you're looking at an ongoing project, and one that will keep changing and growing with you.

5. Bringing life to your habitat garden

But ask the beasts, and they will teach you,
Or the birds of the air, and they will tell you.
FROM THE BOOK OF JOB, CHAPTER 12 VERSE 7

Birds

One of the great joys of growing native plants is watching and listening to the variety of birds that visit, feed or even nest in your garden. Whether it's a pardalote calling from its treetop perch or a flock of raucous yellow-tailed black cockatoos dropping by to tear some bark off your gum trees, each avian caller has its own fascinating characteristics.

This section looks at how to attract birds to your garden, and how to keep them coming back. There are also some important issues associated with having birds in your garden that need to be considered.

The first step towards attracting birds to a garden is to find out a bit about them. Which birds visit the garden? What are their seasonal comings and goings, their diet or their nesting needs? Do they even belong in your garden? It won't be helpful

A striking close-up of a male brown goshawk. These skilful flyers can surprise their prey – other birds and small mammals – by flying suddenly from behind cover. (*Peter Tonelli*)

to the 'locals' if you end up attracting and helping feral species. For instance, starlings have been introduced here and are causing havoc among the local bird species. They are not a species anyone would want to give any advantage to in a habitat garden.

You can learn a lot about birds by watching and taking notes or photographs of them. You can also shortcut your research by contacting a bird observers group, or similar, in your area. For contact details, see p. 51 at the end of this section.

How to attract birds to your garden

Surveys by groups such as Bird Observers Club of Australia (BOCA) have shown that there are five important factors in attracting and keeping birds coming into your habitat garden.

1. Providing food

Birds range from being meat eaters to seed feeders, from insect gobblers and fruit pickers to grub grabbers and nectar sippers. And some birds combine two or more of these eating habits. If your habitat garden is to provide for a variety of birds, it will need to have some of these natural sources of food nearby.

Nectar-rich plants such as grevilleas, banksias and melaleucas are a great starting point, but you need to consider a wider range of foods if you want a wider range of birds than, say, honeyeaters. Insects and other invertebrates are another great attraction for birds. Fortunately most nectar-producing plants also attract insects, which in turn provide food for insectivorous birds, and other animals.

Add any of the vast range of seeding plants to the mix, ranging from wattles to native grasses, and you're well on the way to providing a balanced diet for your avian friends. Basically a good complex plant mix, with some variety in height and type, will mimic a natural habitat. BOCA surveys have also stressed the importance of tall trees that are indigenous to the local area. As well as providing food, they provide shelter and nest sites.

2. Providing water

Water in one form or another is essential for all birds. While some will get it indirectly through their food, most birds require a supply of fresh water for both drinking and washing. By providing a reliable supply of water, you will keep birds in your garden rather than watching them go elsewhere for it.

The minimalist approach is to simply provide places where natural rainwater can collect and remain longer than it does elsewhere. This is well suited to places with regular rainfall. Any dip or low point in your garden could be put to this purpose. By digging it out a bit and giving it a waterproof base, you will enhance the hollow's capacity and the length of time water will remain there. Shading it with plants will also help.

A more active approach is to provide water artificially via a birdbath or something similar. Many birdbaths and garden ponds are commercially available, but you can just as easily rig up your own. If you don't want to make a formal birdbath, you could try using a dripper system whereby water is channelled into a small collecting area or pool. Alternatively allow birds access to a larger pond that has shallow sections suitable for bathing. Islands and shallows within a pond system can also help to safeguard birds against cat attack.

Whatever way you choose to supplement the water supply for birds, there are a few rules of thumb to bear in mind:

Keep it fresh. For the health of the birds that use it, it's important that the water is fresh, and keep it that way.

Make it deep enough. There should be sufficient water for at least small birds to bath in it.

Keep it protected. You don't want your birdbath to become a bloodbath. Keep it protected from attack by cats and other predators. If the birdbath is on a stem or column, you could use a collar around the stem to stop cats climbing. You also could fence off the entire birdbath area.

3. Providing refuge

As well as providing a variety of food, your garden should offer places of refuge. Birds seek shelter from sun, rain and wind as well as from competitors and predators. Dense and prickly plant foliage is the most obvious material to provide such shelter. Variety is the other key; a range of foliage types and heights will best provide for the variety of birds you hope to attract.

Foliage isn't the only form of shelter you can offer. Sometimes a building such as a garden shed or shade house will provide a temporary refuge for birds. Trellises and screens, allied with nearby trees, can give birds the kind of semi-invisibility they require.

4. Providing nesting

Each bird species has a different nesting strategy. Some birds are ground-nesting, some build twiggy platforms in trees, others use hollows or holes. Knowing the nesting needs of the birds in your area will help you to provide the kinds of foliage, nesting materials and physical spaces they want.

Something as simple as leaving a dead tree standing in your garden – if it is safe to do so – may mean the difference between a parrot staying and nesting in your garden or going elsewhere. Look at your garden from a 'bird's eye view' to help you to choose what to plant where, what to remove and what to leave. Always remember that your garden is a finite resource. Just as you can't grow every plant you'd like to, neither will you be able to provide every form of nesting material.

If you want to find out more about the nesting needs of particular birds in your area, contact your local bird observers group, Birds Australia or the Gould League. For contact details see p. 51 at the end of this section.

5. Limiting threats

The greatest threat to birds is humans. Not only do we clear the vegetation that provides them with their nesting, perching and food sources, but we also poison their air, water and food sources. The best we can do for birds is to limit or undo these wrongs, which is one of the main points of having a habitat garden.

Pesticides and other poisons are a danger to birds either through direct ingestion or through a contaminated food chain. DDT's effect on the thinning of egg shells is one of the most notorious examples from the past, but many chemicals can have sinister impacts on all bird populations. A recent study in the United States examined of 80,000 dead birds handed in to wildlife authorities in New York State. It was found that the leading cause of death was pesticide poisoning. The most common of those deadly pesticides were lawn care chemicals.

But even the provision of bird-friendly plants and the non-use of chemicals doesn't end the threats that birds face when they visit your garden. Domestic pets are another powerful threat. The household cat, curled up on your lap in front of a lovely warm fire, might look harmless but it is probably an even more serious threat to birds than pesticides (see pp. 41–42). Even physical rubbish, particularly plastics, can be detrimental to birds as they may ingest it or get caught in it. Each year many birds, especially sea birds, are found entangled in plastic, sometimes fatally. The habitat gardener should be aware of all such threats and minimise their possible impact in the local area.

Once you've started attracting the birds to your garden you need to keep the following issues in mind to maintain a healthy bird habitat.

To feed or not to feed?

The question of whether to supplement the food for the birds in your garden is a difficult one. The ideal is that birds will find all that they need from the resources provided by your garden and the local area. There's a good chance that past practices in your neighbourhood, such as removal of native vegetation, have reduced their food supply. Some of these birds need every little bit of help they can get.

There may also be events such as storms or a hard frost that create a special short-term food shortage. Finally, there's the educational value, and indeed the sheer pleasure, of watching birds at a feed table. Every gardener needs to weigh up the pros and cons to make their own decision. If you do decide to supplement the feed of birds in your garden, there are a few things to keep in mind.

Don't kill them with kindness

By keeping artificial feeding to a minimum, at a supplementary level only, you are ensuring that birds don't become used to being fed by you. Over-generous feeding over a long period of time puts them at risk if you are away for any length of time, or if you move.

Give them the right food

Although not all birds eat the same things, there are some good standbys for the major common food types, such as nectar, grains and 'puddings'. Contact your local council, WIRES or your local bird group for any information on food for different species.

Welcoming the swallows

Welcome Swallows and Fairy Martins are found in most parts of Australia. They build mud nests under eaves and bridges or on cliffs, banks and similar surfaces. If you want them to build their nests in your garden in spring, you'll need to offer a supply of mud or clay, plus some suitable nesting surfaces. If they're going to stay around they'll also need a supply of food suitable for themselves and their chicks. The gardener lucky enough to have swallows or martins will find that they love flies and mosquitos, and eat them in vast quantities.

Offer variety

Most birds vary their diet according to the season and the availability of food types. Research has shown, for example, that nectar feeders such as New Holland Honeyeaters can become ill if they rely too heavily on just nectar. (They also need insects in their diet.) The ideal for the home bird feeder is to know what your birds eat when, and to adjust your feeding regime accordingly. Seek expert help from bird groups if you need it.

Keep it clean

A bird feeder can become the source of cross-infection from one bird to another. By cleaning out the feeders regularly, and by keeping food levels low, you limit the risk of spreading disease.

Protect the feeder

There are ways to make sure your feed table for birds doesn't become a dining table for cats. Suspending the tray or table from a tree branch is one way to help, putting a collar or hood around the tree trunk is another. You can also use a metal, or similar slippery material, pole for the feeder as cats can't climb such slender or slippery surfaces.

Nestboxes: pros and cons

The thought of having birds breeding and nesting in our own backyards is a very attractive one. There is great joy, and sometimes sorrow, in watching a bird family go through the trials of mating, laying, brooding, hatching, feeding and fledging. Gardeners who provide nestboxes for birds give themselves the chance to witness these things.

Yet some of the issues that apply to artificial feeding also apply to artificial nestboxes. Ideally you would want enough old trees and tree-hollows in your neighbourhood for birds to nest in. But in most gardens that is unlikely, due to often thoughtless removal of nesting habitat. The idea of supplementing nesting places takes on a stronger imperative, and given that some birds will help themselves to parts of our houses for nesting anyway, for example, Welcome Swallows plastering their mud nests under our eaves, we might as well make it easy for them.

Again there are some practical matters to bear in mind when putting in nestboxes.

Location, location

As with human housing, the placement of a nestbox can make all the difference. The box needs to be as waterproof as possible, preferably facing away from prevailing rain-bearing winds. It is best placed in a shady or semi-shady position at least 2m above ground level for most birds. It should also be near sources of food and water. Remember that you will need access to the box, so place it where you'll at least be able to watch it or, if not, where you can climb to it easily.

Design is important

The box needs to be sturdy, and strongly attached to prevent predators from dislodging it. The use of tree collars will also help keep cats and rats out. Also one size *doesn't* fit all when it comes to nestboxes. Each bird species has particular nest needs. You can learn this by trial and error but you'll save a lot of effort, and help the birds more effectively, if you contact groups such as Bird Observers

(BOCA) or Birds Australia. They can provide nestbox and other information for many local native species. Examples of nestboxes can be found at: www.birdobservers.org.au/nestboxes.htm

Actively monitor the box
You need to keep an eye on what's happening inside nestboxes. They can easily play host to introduced or unwanted birds, invertebrates or even rats. Starlings and mynahs are a particular problem in much of eastern Australia, especially as they often out-compete local native birds. The last thing you want to do is provide introduced pests with yet another advantage over the locals. Remove and destroy the eggs or nestlings of unwanted species if you discover them in your nestbox. Take the same action, carefully, with rats, wasps or honeybees.

Quite a number of birds, many of them threatened species, use tree-hollows for nesting, and one of the best things you can do in your habitat garden is to have trees mature enough to develop hollows. If you're starting a garden from scratch this isn't possible, but for any other gardener it means that a special value should be placed on old trees already in the garden.

Some birds that use tree-hollows
Ducks (some species sometimes)
Falcons
Cockatoos (all species)
Parrots (many species)
Hawk Owls
Barn Owls (some species)
Owlet Nightjars
Tree Kingfishers and Kookaburras (some species)
Treecreepers
Scrubwrens, Gerygones, Thornbills and allies
Sparrows, Grass Finches and Mannikins (most species)
Swallows and Martins (some nests)
Starlings and Mynahs (introduced species)

* Information courtesy of Bird Observers Club of Australia

When native birds become a problem: swooping magpies
Magpies are renowned for dive-bombing anyone entering their territory during the breeding and nesting season. They may actually peck at the heads of people walking by, and can sometimes draw blood.

Birds and windows: a clear danger

Windows, glass doors or any large glass area can be a hazard to flying birds. If they can see daylight through the glass, birds will often fly straight into it, thinking they're going straight to the daylight on the other side. Glass strike can kill or injure a bird. There are simple and effective ways to reduce the hazard.

Put a bird of prey cut-out on potentially dangerous windows. This will distract the gaze of flying birds from what's beyond the window.

Locate a birdbath quite close to the window. As well as giving you a great view of your avian visitors, it will slow down birds flying by. And birds drinking/bathing at it will not be flying at maximum speed nearby.

Grow bushes near the window to slow down 'through-flyers'.

To protect yourself and/or deter further swoops:
- avoid the area where magpies are swooping and make a temporary sign to inform others;
- wear a hat while in the area;
- carry an open umbrella;
- carry a stick or branch above your head.

Don't stop if you are attacked. You're still in the bird's territory, so it will keep trying to warn you off. Walk quickly out of the area.

An aggressive Magpie should NOT be removed from the area for a number of reasons. First, the eggs will fail to hatch or the young will die of starvation and exposure. If a territory is vacated, other magpies from less suitable areas will claim it and build new nests of their own. If only the nest is removed the birds will simply build another one in the same area. It's best to learn to live with these beautiful birds. You'll enjoy their singing and the antics of the fledglings. In return give them a bit of space during the breeding season.

More information on birds in the garden

Birds Australia
National Office and Library:
(open Monday–Friday 9am–5pm)
415 Riversdale Rd,
Hawthorn East VIC 3123
Phone: (03) 9882 2622
Fax: (03) 9882 2677
Email: mail@birdsaustralia.com.au
Web: www.birdsaustralia.com.au

Bird Observers Club of Australia
183–185 Springvale Road,
Nunawading VIC 3131
Phone: 1300 305 342 (toll-free within Australia) or (03) 9877 5342
Fax: (03) 9894 4048
Email: boca@ozemail.com.au
Web: www.birdobservers.org.au

Mammals

Gutteral wheezes
and the scourscream
of old kitchens
Hushed, staring over their shoulders,
they reflect torch glare
With eyes quizzical and cautious.
Blunt warriors;
bane of rose-fanciers
In fringe suburbs
FROM 'POSSUM' BY JAMES CHARLTON FROM
LUMINOUS BODIES.

Australia has a unique array of mammals. Our fauna is one of the wonders of the natural world, something so special, so different, that early European naturalists spoke of Australia being 'a separate creation'. Yet of all the extinctions that have taken place here since Europeans arrived, mammals have suffered the most. Despite this, the average Australian gardener knows little or nothing about our native mammals. Perhaps the vision of ill-informed foreigners who imagine kangaroos hopping about our streets and gardens has some merit. Is it really so strange to expect that our native animals might form part of the fauna in our gardens? What could be more wonderful than having a koala up your gum tree or a Barred Bandicoot in your bushes? As well as giving you a thrill, our mammals play a number of vital roles in keeping our native bush in natural balance. Mammals help to pollinate many plants, keep invertebrate pest numbers down, naturally prune our vegetation, disperse seeds, aerate and fertilise our soil, recycle waste materials and generally contribute in many ways. In short if you want a balanced ecosystem, they're essential to have around.

This section looks at how you can attract mammals to your garden, and keep them coming back. There are also some important issues associated with having mammals in your garden that need to be considered.

First it's important to find out which native mammals actually live in your neighbourhood. One way you can do this is by making your own careful observations. As most of our mammals are crepuscular (active at dusk and dawn) or nocturnal (active at night), these are the best times to try and spy on them. Spotlighting is one good way of seeing what's about at night, though you should be aware that bright lights can disturb native animals. The use of a red filter (or red cellophane) over your light or torch will reduce the disturbance.

However it is also possible to discover what's been active in your local area by looking for animal signs during daylight hours. In my own garden I discovered the presence of bandicoots before I ever saw them. Their telltale conical diggings in my lawn gave away their nighttime presence. I was able to confirm it by finding some scats (animal faeces) that were identified as having come from an Eastern Barred Bandicoot.

Other animals give away their presence by leaving 'runways', where parts of the bush are pressed into small paths or tunnels by the repeated passing of animal feet. The size of this runway or some fur or droppings along the path can also give clues to the identity of the animal.

Of course it isn't always difficult to know which native animal is about. Most Australians know when they have possums, especially Brushtailed Possums, because of their habit of running about on the roof, and sometimes getting under it. Possums also leave territorial marks on trees, often by tearing at the bark. And they can wreak havoc in vegetable and fruit gardens, but more about that later.

Harder to spot are the less common Ringtailed Possum, and the even smaller varieties of Pygmy Possums and gliders. And there are dozens of other lesser-known native species that may be found around your neighbourhood. Depending on where you live, you might have creatures as exotic as phascogales, antechinuses, bettongs, woylies or wombats. While the list isn't quite endless, you might be surprised at how many animals there are. (See *Complete Book of Australian Mammals* by R. Strahan (ed.) published in 1991 by Angus & Robertson.)

Apart from doing your own detective work, another way to find out what shares the neighbourhood with you is to go to the experts. In most regions the local office of your National Parks and Wildlife Service or Environment Department should be able to help with your enquiry.

Bats should get special mention here, but first let's clear something up. 'Vampires!' There, I've said it, and got it out of the way. Our poor bats have always been at the unfashionable end of the animal spectrum, and the dracula/vampire thing is largely to blame for this irrational downgrading. Bats are actually mammals. They do NOT suck blood from humans, at least not in Australia. Rather, depending on the species, they eat either fruit or invertebrates.

Bats play a vital part in the environment by keeping insect pest numbers down, sometimes in spectacular fashion. Recent research in Queensland showed that one colony of 250,000 Bent-winged Bats ate an incredible 1 tonne of insects in a year. Fruit bats and flying foxes are also vital to the pollination and seed dispersal of native forest trees, as well as introduced crop plants. But apart from performing such valuable environmental services they are also marvellous to watch as they fly around at dusk, using their extraordinary sonar-like navigation system.

Unfortunately bats are extremely vulnerable to a number of human activities. Habitat removal and the use of pesticides on their food and/or nesting places are among the most damaging things we can do to these animals. Developing a carefully managed habitat garden is one of the most helpful things we can do.

How to attract mammals to your garden

The important factors in attracting and keeping mammals are similar to those for birds, though there are some significant differences.

Sugar gliders need trees and the food sources found in trees to survive and thrive. They eat a surprising variety of foods, including sap, gum, nectar and insects. (*Peter Tonelli*)

Providing food

If you want to 'target' particular species for your garden, why not do some research and find out what food different species prefer to eat, and then provide it.

Nectar-rich plants are a good start as they provide direct food for some species, such as gliders, and indirect food for other animals. For instance, nectar-producing plants also attract insects, which in turn provide food for insectivorous mammals.

Providing water

All mammals need water. Providing a reliable supply of water in your garden is an effective way to help keep animals there rather than going elsewhere in search of it.

As previously mentioned, the simplest approach is to provide places where natural rainwater can be collected and remain longer than it does elsewhere in the garden. This technique is well suited to places with regular rainfall. Any dip or low point in your garden could be put to this purpose. Dig it out a little and give the hollow a waterproof base; shading it with plants will also help keep the area moist and cool.

Of course that's halfway towards a formal pond, and given that animals aren't fussy about appearances, it's just as likely that a formal pool will be visited by a thirsty native animal as an informal pool, especially under cover of darkness. See pp. 72–73 for more information on how to create your own multipurpose pond in the 'Aquatic animals' section in Chapter 5.

Providing refuge

As well as providing a variety of food, incorporate in your garden places of refuge. Mammals find clumping plants and bushes particularly suitable as places of refuge from competitors and predators. In my own garden a variety of clumping plants shelter the resident bandicoot population from cats and dogs, their main enemies. Non-native vegetation is good for providing cover so don't remove it all when you are providing a refuge garden, replace it gradually. Recent research in Tasmania has shown that some non-native plants, including the dreaded gorse, are as good as some native bushes in providing cover. (Of course there are other reasons for resisting the use of gorse, though it is a wise precaution to be sure that replacement shelter bushes are available before removing all gorse plants.) I've also found that possums, brushtailed and ringtailed, will take refuge in plants as diverse as conifers and climbers like honeysuckle.

Providing nesting

As well as sheltering in bushes, some mammals nest in them. Others use hollows or holes in taller trees, or grassy nests on the ground. Knowing the nesting needs of the mammals in your area will help you to provide the kinds of foliage, nesting materials and physical spaces they want. As with birds, artificial nestboxes can be used.

Limiting threats

Humans and their pets are the greatest threat to native mammals. However we can minimise or eliminate these threats in our habitat garden. See pp. 41–42 on how to minimise the threat from cats in the 'Threats to the habitat garden' section in Chapter 4.

Flying foxes: a special case

Flying foxes are the largest and most visible of Australia's bats, yet their populations are under threat right across Australia. Those who see vast numbers against the evening skies of northern and eastern Australia, or orchardists who count the cost of crop damage inflicted by them, may laugh at such a claim. But studies over the last several decades indicate widespread and drastic decline in their numbers, most of it caused by habitat loss.

While a whole colony of flying foxes in your garden may be beyond your hopes (or wishes) it is possible for a habitat garden to attract these larger bats, and to provide for some of their needs.

Food plants for flying foxes

Blossoming and fruiting native plants are the key to the flying fox diet. A wide range of flowering eucalypts that are suitable for gardens will provide food for flying foxes. These include: *Eucalyptus melliodora, E. alba, E. curtisii, E. microcorys, E. robusta,* and *E. tessellaris.* In very large gardens taller species such as *E. obliqua, E. camaldulensis, E. viminalis, E. botryoides, E. andrewsii* or *E. terreticornis* could be tried. This last tree is also an important food plant for koalas, but as it grows to 50m, it will only suit spacious gardens. Other flying fox food plants include many in the fig family (for example, *Ficus obliqua, F. fraseri* and *F. coronata*), some taller grevilleas (for example, *Grevillea robusta, G. pteridifolia*), taller paperbarks (for example, *Melaleuca leucodendron, M. quinquenervia* and *M. viridiflora*), *Melia azedarach* (white cedar) and some of *Syzygium* species (lilly pillies).

Food plants for koalas

One of the world's favourite animals has to be the koala. This tree-dwelling marsupial, closely related to the wombat, has developed a very specialised diet. It consists almost entirely of leaves from a limited number of native trees, most of them eucalypts. Their diet does vary from place to place and season to season. However if you live in an area that's inhabited by koalas, and you have the right mature trees, it is possible that you could host them in your garden, and what better reward for creating a good habitat could there be than that? Koala plant foods include *Eucalyptus* species such as *camaldulensis, globulus, haemastoma, maculata, melliodora, obliqua, platypus, rubida, saligna* and *viminalis*, plus *Lophostemon confertus*, among others.

When native animals become pests

Many Australians are familiar with the nocturnal roof rumblings of Brushtail Possums. They are probably the most comfortably urban of all our native mammals, at home in our ceilings and wall cavities, happy munching on the vegetables, fruit, foliage and flowers in our gardens. While some people might count this as a sign of their success in habitat gardening, not all will enjoy the possum's attentions.

Fortunately there are ways of successfully sharing your garden with possums. Two important things you can do are to provide alternative nesting spaces and protect your vegetable, fruit and flower gardens.

Providing alternative nesting spaces

Possums are highly territorial, so trapping and removing them from one area to another often results in their being out-competed by possums already living there.

If local possums are causing you sleepless nights by nesting in your roof, the most humane solution is to provide an alternative nesting area nearby. Sometimes a disused outbuilding such as the woodshed or garden shed might suffice, although a purpose-built possum box placed in a tree or on a high wall away from the house is probably the best solution. Once you have built the alternative nest, you are ready to transfer the possums to their new home.

Possum nests are made up of twigs, bark and other natural materials. The nesting material will carry the possum's scent, so taking it away to the new nest box will encourage the transfer. Possums are active at night, so it's best to locate and remove nesting material from your roof at night while they are away. After you've set up the new nest, you might entice possums into it by placing some food, for example, banana or apple, near the entrance of the new nest. Once you are sure the possums are no longer in your roof, block any entry points into your ceiling or wall cavity. Again, do this at night when the possums are away from their nest. Splash the entry points of the old nest with a strong smelling substance such as camphor or naphthalene to further deter the newly evicted possum.

Protecting your vegetable, fruit and flower gardens

The surest way to keep possums out of your vegetable, fruit or flower garden is to fence it completely. A fence that includes a roof cover is the most effective, but this can be expensive and time consuming to build. A 1.5m high wire fence with a floppy top will do just as well. Use heavily galvanised chicken wire that is higher than you need, say 1.8m. Dig a trench about 20cm deep around the perimeter of your garden. Put the chicken wire into the trench to a depth of 20cm and bury the bottom of it in the ground, turning it

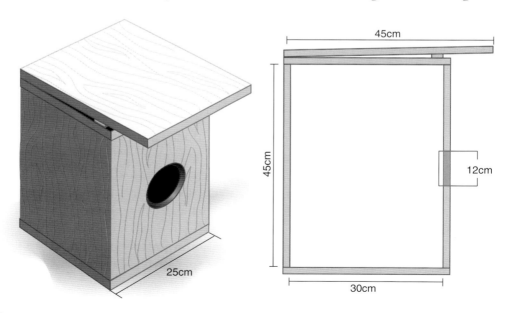

A simple possum nesting-box design.

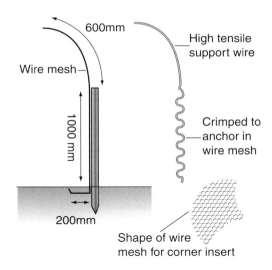

A floppy fence design. The wire curves outwards away from the garden.

outwards to deter digging. Support the wire on posts to a height of about 1m, as for a normal fence. Curve the top 60cm or so outwards, supporting it with lengths of high-tensile wire at regular intervals. Possums don't like climbing wire, but will climb up the posts of conventional fences. However the wire crescent at the top of this floppy fence will deter possums.

Netting fruit trees is another alternative and it has the advantage of keeping birds off the fruit as well. Bird scarers can also work with possums, though a loud scarer going off at night will not endear you to your neighbours.

Other possum repellents include:
- blood and bone at the base of plants;
- egg powder, mixed with water and a wetting agent, sprayed on plants;
- mutton fat and kerosene. Mix nine parts of melted mutton fat with one part of kerosene and apply to the stems and lower branches of affected plants. Avoid applying it to leaves, as it may burn some species.

Some gardeners report good success with the use of Quassia chips. These are derived from a plant in the genus *Quassia*, which is native to South America. Quassia has long been used for medicinal purposes, especially *Q. amara*, whose wood, bark and root segments are used as a health tonic and insecticide. Quassia is considered gentle to the environment, has a short residual life, and readily breaks down. It can be used in either spray or chip form as an effective natural possum deterrent. It can be purchased from many hardware stores and some pharmacies.

A recipe for Quassia spray is to add 100g of quassia chips to 400ml of boiling water. Allow the mix to stand for 5 minutes before adding one litre of cold water. Leave for 24 hours, then strain and

What's that noise in the ceiling?

Possums aren't the only animals that can disturb your rest by their nighttime activities in your roof space. Rodents often share our living spaces too. The best way to be sure is to look in your ceiling space with a torch during the night. If you're still not sure you've got a possum, try this checklist.

- Rodents (rats and mice) make scratching, gnawing and skittering noises
- Rodents sometimes chew electrical wiring
- Rats and mice have smaller pellet-like droppings, whereas possums have larger faeces which are sometimes joined together in lumps
- Rats often collect seeds and grasses for their nests, and never defaecate in their nests
- Possums make loud, heavy thumping sounds when walking, and growls, coughs or screeches when disturbed.

add a wetting agent. Spray onto plants or in areas where you want to keep possums away. Quassia spray may have to be reapplied frequently as it breaks down readily, especially in wet weather.

For more information on animal habitats, nesting boxes and what to feed native animals, you can contact Wildlife Information and Rescue Service (WIRES) in NSW on 1800 641 188 or (02) 8977 3333. See their website at: www.wires.com.au/index.html for links to a number of similar groups in the rest of Australia.

Insects and other invertebrates

Greetings, spiders, with whom we inhabit common space;
and potoroo and magpie, also having a part in us, and we with you.
Greetings to everyday epiphanies;
not forgetting you insects,
in bodiliness our brothers
FROM 'SISTER SPIDER' BY JAMES CHARLTON IN LUMINOUS BODIES.

Whenever you walk on a piece of ground, you pass over thousands of invertebrates (animals without backbones) with every step. Research in natural grasslands in eastern Australia has shown that there is an estimated average of 140kg of invertebrates per hectare. And that's just the easily seen larger invertebrates such as earthworms, millipedes, centipedes and larvae. Invertebrates include spiders, moths, butterflies, snails and slugs.

This huge number and variety of invertebrates benefits the environment in many ways. Being such a diverse group of animals there's an invertebrate for practically every task from plant pollination and waste recycling to scavenging and food production. These tasks might not sound very important but the environmental and economical benefits are priceless. For example, look at pollination. Without moths, beetles, native bees, flies and other invertebrates performing their pollinating job, few of our food crops, fruiting and flowering plants would be able to reproduce. While pollination by hand is possible, the importance of invertebrates would become clearer if we had to pollinate every single food plant or flower ourselves.

Invertebrates are also a crucial link in the food chain. Virtually every other type of animal, from birds and mammals to reptiles and amphibians, depends on insects for food. Even those that don't devour insects directly, for example leaf, grass and fruit eaters, depend on the pollinating work of insects for their meals. For all of these reasons a good habitat garden needs to attract and retain a wide variety of invertebrates.

So how do you go about doing this? This can be a little difficult. Compared with birds and mammals, less is known about invertebrates and their specific needs. So attracting them to your garden may not be as predictable a process as it is with other animals.

Arguably our best-loved invertebrates, the butterflies, provide a good example of both our ignorance and our knowledge. Along with moths they share the order of insects known as *Lepidoptera*. There are more than 20,000 Australian species in the order, with butterflies making up only about 400 of that number. Butterflies tend to live in warmer and wetter areas, so the tropics have the highest concentration,

> ### War or peace with insects?
>
> Some might ask why you would want to actually attract insects into your garden. After all, isn't humankind at virtual war with anything that creeps, crawls or buzzes? My father used to tell the story of how he once followed a large and beautiful butterfly into a neighbour's yard to photograph it. As he arrived the neighbour was just returning from the bottom of the yard with a can of insect spray and a satisfied look. 'I just took care of that pesky insect,' she beamed to my incredulous father.
>
> Despite such feelings towards them, the fact is that invertebrates, animals without backbones, are a vital part of every ecosystem. In fact invertebrates outnumber any other life form on the planet. Our dislike of flies, mosquitos and cockroaches shouldn't blind us to the habitat benefits these amazingly diverse creatures can bring to our gardens.

although most areas in Australia have at least some butterflies.

There are two main approaches to take when attracting invertebrates to your garden. First, you can focus on good general habitat gardening practices. Second, you can learn something about the ecology of or the relationship between the particular species of invertebrates that could potentially live in your garden.

Understanding the ecology and behaviour of invertebrates

Butterflies and moths in the garden

Attracting butterflies to your garden involves providing for them throughout their lifecycle, especially at the distinctive caterpillar and butterfly stages.

There are many native plant species with flowers that will attract feeding butterflies, or foliage that will provide food or cover. Otherwise butterflies and moths would never have thrived in Australia.

Following is a list of some commonly found native plants that may encourage the presence of butterflies and moths in Australian gardens.

Ants in the garden

Humans have always been fascinated, and sometimes irritated, by ants. Their vast numbers and seeming tirelessness make them big players in most habitats. There are more than 1,500 different species of ants to be found in Australia. While they occur in all climates and ecosystems, ants have a particular affinity for trees. While

> ### Moth or butterfly: what's the difference?
>
> The difference between these two members of the order *Lepidoptera* is fairly technical. Basically butterflies are moths which:
> - have clubbed antennae;
> - are day-flyers;
> - usually sit with their wings upright;
> - lack a wing-coupling spine (frenulum) on their hind wing.
>
> In many other ways moths and butterflies have remarkably similar life cycles. It is certainly not true that moths are the 'ugly ducklings' of the order, as many moths can be as colourful and strikingly marked as any butterfly. Perhaps their tendency towards night flight means that we don't see these beautiful winged insects as often as their day flying colleagues.

only some ant species nest in trees, many more use trees as larders and hunt for nectar and invertebrate prey in every part of the tree. While they do this ants perform a couple of vital habitat roles, pollination and pest eradication. Ants also help with the germination of small seeded plants, which they often carry into their ground nests, where some of the seeds take root. They also aerate the soil and introduce new materials which can enrich the soil.

Every garden, habitat garden or not, will have ants. Here are a few tips to go the next step and actually welcome them:
- leave soil undisturbed (where possible);
- grow nectar-rich plants;
- grow trees;
- don't use poisons in the garden;
- encourage a diversity of plants and animals within your garden.

Dragonflies in the garden

Few invertebrates have the aerial skill and graceful presence of the dragonfly.

The life cycle of a butterfly

The life cycle of a typical butterfly illustrates the complexity of its habitat needs. Adult butterflies are generally nectar feeders, so they require flowering plants (often quite specific types for each species) during that phase of their life. They also take up nutrients from such sources as water, mud puddles, fruit and animal droppings.

The butterfly phase is only one part of a long process that starts when the male of the species tracks down the female via the scent (pheromone) she releases. After mating, the female butterfly lays a cluster of eggs, sometimes numbering in the thousands, on the leaves of a plant on which the hatched larvae will feed. The larvae, commonly called caterpillars, feed and grow, shedding their skins (exoskeletons) four or five times to enable room for growth. They finally pupate, usually hanging as a chrysalis beneath a leaf, before emerging as an adult butterfly. This whole process, from egg to butterfly, will have taken anything from a few weeks to a few years. It will have required a variety of different plants, a number of other specific habitat features, and not a bit of luck in avoiding predators.

If that life-cycle description loosely fits just 400 or so of the 20,000 *Lepidoptera*, and there are closer to 90,000 insect species (not to mention all the other invertebrates) in the country, you can see how incredibly complex the matter of invertebrate habitats can become.

The bark shed from this eucalypt makes an ideal shelter for invertebrates and skinks. (*Ian Jeanneret*)

> **Attractive, but . . .**
>
> Attracting butterflies to your garden is one thing. Doing it in a way that enhances the general habitat of your garden and neighbourhood is another. For example, the introduced plant *Lantana camara* is an excellent source of nectar for butterflies, but in many parts of Australia is also a disastrously successful invasive weed. Lantana could never be recommended for the Australian habitat garden.

Dragonflies, and their relatives the damsel flies, are both members of the *Odonata* order, which contains around 300 different species in Australia. Contrary to popular belief these 'flies' don't sting and cannot harm humans in any way.

While dragonflies will venture away from water, their whole life cycle, as well as their favourite foods, revolve around the presence of standing fresh water. So a pond is one of the most important ingredients for attracting dragonflies into your garden. They lay their eggs in water and the larvae (sometimes known as mudeye) live in water through 10 to 15 moults, preying upon a wide variety of aquatic life, including mosquito wrigglers. The larval phase, which can last over a year, ends when the final larva, or nymph, crawls out of the water onto the stem of an aquatic plant or a rock, and emerges from its case as an adult dragonfly. This usually happens at night and can be observed by torchlight.

Dragonflies hunt on the wing and catch small flying insects, especially mosquitos, with great success. The aerobatic skills of the dragonflies are due, in part, to their wing configuration. They have a pair of wings on either side of their body. These wings are independent and don't come together during flight. This enables dragonflies to manoeuvre very tightly, to

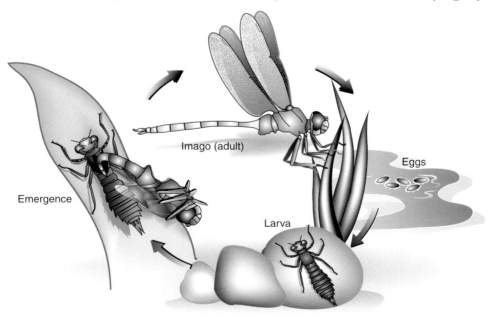

Life cycle of a dragonfly.

> **How dragonflies and damsel flies differ**
>
> Dragonflies and damsel flies have very similar body shapes, colours and life cycles. The easiest way to tell them apart is via their wings. Dragonfly wings are always held horizontally, perpendicular to the body when at rest. Damsel fly wings are more slender, and they are held into their bodies when at rest.

hover over water, and even fly backwards. They are a sight worth taking the time to see, and a superb addition to any habitat garden.

Apart from having a healthy garden pond, the other main thing you can do to provide habitat for dragonflies and damsel flies is to supply good aquatic and fringing plants in and around the pond. Dragonfly eggs are often laid on submerged plant stems, and the nymphs eventually use these to emerge from the water. Adult dragonflies often perch on the stems of plants near a pond so they can survey the scene with their huge compound eyes.

Spiders in the garden

If you have mixed feelings about spiders, and it's fair to say that few people count them among their friends, you are not alone. On the other hand genuine arachnophobia is relatively rare. So it's probably worth subjecting our mixed feelings to a bit of analysis. Part of our fear undoubtedly comes from the fact that spiders are poisonous. It's true that of the 1500 odd species of spider in Australia, most use venom to kill their prey. However, very few of those species, perhaps 2 per cent in total, have a bite that will present any danger to humans. There are precautions that can be taken that will lessen the threat those few species pose.

It's also worth acknowledging that spiders are everywhere. Through their ability to literally drop in on a line of silk, spiders are among the most successful of colonists. Consequently spiders are present in every garden, as they are in every house and virtually every other place humans find themselves. We have co-existed with them for millennia, despite pesticides and professional exterminators. Spiders are here to stay.

Spiders also play a number of vital roles in the environment. Apart from eating insects and other invertebrates they are, in turn, eaten by birds and mammals (as well as by each other). They are also important pollinators of a number of plant species.

While spider beauty may be in the eye of the beholder, few will refuse to admit that a dew bedecked spider web is one of the marvels of nature. Watching a spider

> **Minimising spider risks**
>
> - Adopt a 'look but don't touch' approach;
> - Learn to tell your local spiders apart;
> - Learn to respect rather than fear spiders. Teach your children the same;
> - Avoid walking barefoot around the garden at night;
> - Don't leave clothes lying around on the floor;
> - Check shoes/boots before putting them on
> - Use gloves when gardening;
> - Don't try to kill spiders unless absolutely necessary (and note that spray insecticides are often ineffective against spiders).

The sparse but prickly foliage of this wattle (*Acacia tetragonophylla*) offers ideal protection for nesting zebra finches.

Coming ready or not. A Welcome Swallow has built its nest under the eaves of a new building, which mimic an overhanging riverbank or cliff.

A habitat woodpile can be home or host to fungi, algae, mosses, lichens, invertebrates, reptiles, birds, amphibians and mammals. The messier the better – from the wildlife's point-of-view.

A fallen tree becomes a horizontal larder for hundreds of invertebrates, and eventually many other life forms.

The Southern Boobook is another commonly heard owl found throughout the country, especially in and near woodland. They nest in tree-hollows; the juvenile in this photograph is about to outgrow this one. (*Peter Tonelli*)

Masked Owls are night hunters in the mid-storey of forest and woodlands right around the coasts and ranges of Australia. (*Peter Tonelli*)

Hollows – ideal nesting sites for birds and mammals – often form after a tree has lost a limb. Although this blue gum (*E. globulus*) is too large for most gardens, many smaller mature trees provide similar habitat niches.

Students learn about nestboxes first hand. This box – designed for galahs – will be used as a temporary measure until natural nesting spaces develop in the new planting. (*Mark Butz*)

A common suburban-dweller all over Australia is the Brushtail Possum. While preferring tree-hollows, the species has adapted well to the roof spaces of our buildings. (*Peter Tonelli*)

Ringtail Possums are less common in the suburbs than Brushtails. This is partly because they prefer continuous tree cover in moving from place to place, and urban areas don't always provide this. Dense foliage, tree-hollows, and roof spaces are used for nesting and shelter. (*Peter Tonelli*)

A floppy fence protects a newly planted area from foraging possums and wallabies. Note how the outward curved section of chicken wire is loosely held in place by a length of curved high-tensile wire. Possums will climb rigid fences, including fence posts, but do not like the movements made by a floppy fence.

Invertebrate heaven – a paperbark in bloom.

A kunzia in bloom – bliss for bugs.

This Case Moth larva (or caterpillar) specialises in eating eucalypt leaves. After pupating it will emerge as a moth and will lay its eggs only on certain types of eucalypt leaves. (*Peter Tonelli*)

A large Wattle Goat Moth, a cossid moth that's often seen flying around lights at night. Goat Moth larvae bore holes into wattle trees, eating out large tunnels before emerging as mature moths. (*Peter Tonelli*)

A dragonfly – a marvel in any garden that provides food and water for this graceful invertebrate. (*Peter Tonelli*)

Some native plants that attract butterflies and moths

This list contains species from all around Australia. In a habitat garden use only those species that occur naturally in your area.

Species Name	Common Name/s	Species Name	Common Name/s
Acacia species (most)	wattle	*Grevillea* species	grevillea
Actinotus helianthi	flannel flowers	*Hakea* species	hakea
Alphitonia excelsa	red ash	*Hoya* species	hoya
Amyema species	mistletoe	*Hymenanthera dentata*	—
Angophora species	angophora, apple gum	*Hypocalymma* species	—
Aristolochia deltantha	—	*Jacksonia scoparia*	dogwood
Banksia species	banksia	*Jasminum lineare*	native jasmine
Brachychiton species	Kurrajong, Illawarra Flame, bottle tree	*Kunzea* species	kunzia
		Leptospermum species	tea tree
Brachyscome multifida	daisy	*Lomandra* species	lomandra, sagg, mat rushes
Bracteantha bracteata	everlasting daisy, straw flower		
		Lomatia species	wild parsley
Breynia species	—	*Melaleuca* species	paperbark, honey myrtle
Buckinghamia celsissima	ivory curl	*Melicope elleryana*	—
Bursaria species	bursaria, Tasmanian Christmas bush, blackthorn	*Microcitrus* species	native lime
		Micromelum minutum	—
Callicoma serratifolia	blackwattle	*Microlaena stipoides*	—
Callistemon species	bottlebrush	*Morinda* species	—
Calytrix tetragona	fringe myrtle	*Olearia* species	daisy bush, musk
Carex fascicularis	tassel sedge	*Parsonia* species	—
Cassia species (some now *Senna*)	cassia	*Passiflora* species	native passionfruit
		Poa species	poa
Chionochloa species	wallaby grass	*Pomaderris* species	dogwood
Chrysocephalum species	yellow button, paper daisy	*Pultenaea* species	bacon and eggs
Craspedia canens	Billy button	*Senna* species	cassia
Dianella species	flax lily	*Tasmannia* species	pepperbush
Doryanthes species	Gymea lily, spear lily	*Thelionema caespitosa*	—
Eucalyptus species (most)	gum trees	*Wahlenbergia* species	native bluebell
Exocarpus cupressiformis	native cherry	*Wilkiea* species	—

Growing your habitat garden **63**

at work on its web can also be a deeply fascinating pastime. Webs have one additional and quite unusual use. They are often 'borrowed' by birds for use in nest making.

The Sydney Funnel-web spider is our best known venomous spider. Although Funnel-webs are common in many parts of Australia, it's the Sydney sub-species that is considered the most dangerous. Funnel-webs nest in holes in moist, shady areas such as leaf litter, rockeries and shrubberies. They are sometimes driven out of the holes during heavy rain or at mating time, and this is when you are most likely to find them around human dwellings. Gardeners will sometimes disturb them when digging. As the greatest danger comes from spiders if they get inside your house, it's wise to try and exclude them. Fit draught excluders to exterior doors and insect screens to windows and air vents. Keeping a clear area around your doorways will also discourage Funnel-webs from nesting too close to the house.

The Red-back spider is another common, if slightly less venomous spider. A member of the Black Widow family, the Red-back prefers dry, sheltered places for its web-building. It is widely distributed across Australia and is often found in sheds, around woodpiles or in rubbish piles. If Red-backs are present in large numbers in your garden, the best precaution is to keep your shed clean and tidy, and to look out for their webs. These are distinguished by a conical retreat at the top, and a mass of usually vertical threads at the bottom. To remove the web, spiders and all, put on thick gloves and wind the web around a stick or broom handle. Dispose of the spiders – insect spray is effective if applied direct – and watch for new web formation, a sure sign that new spiders have moved in.

The White-tailed spider is another common and sometimes dangerous spider and is found across Australia. They spin no webs, so you'll only know you have them when you see them. They are distinguished by their long black to grey cylindrical abdomen, which tapers to a white tip. They tend to shelter in dark undisturbed areas, such as timber piles in garden sheds, and come out at night to hunt. They will hide in cupboards, in curtains, on towels and other dark sheltered spots if they get inside the house. Remove any spiders you find, and take the precaution of checking shoes, clothing and bedding if these spiders are frequent visitors to your house.

Note: If you are bitten seek medical attention immediately. Try to make a positive identification of the spider, or if it is safe to do so, catch the spider and take it with you.

When an invertebrate isn't an insect

Not every 'creepy crawly' is actually an insect. One of the most common mistakes people make is to call spiders insects. A spider is actually an arachnid, an order that includes scorpions and mites. While arachnids are invertebrates in that they don't have a backbone, they are NOT insects. The main difference is that insects have six legs, while spiders have eight.

In the habitat garden spiders should generally be welcomed. We can do this in a number of ways, including:
- providing places for them to shelter and/or make webs, for example, woodpiles, hollows, leaf litter, etcetera;
- providing food, for example, insects;
- avoiding the use of pesticides.

Amphibians

From tiny tadpoles to wrigglers only slightly bigger,
Sprouting hind legs even as the tail remained to propel,
To nourish, the toadlets oversummered in our sunny tubs.
Eventually, they graduated to air and our congratulations.
We cheered them on in their safaris through the uncut lawn
FROM 'BIRTH OF A NATURALIST' BY LOUISE FABIANI IN *THE GREEN ALEMBIC*.

Tadpoles and frogs have always held a fascination for children. If we're truthful, the same is probably true for most adults. Who hasn't marvelled at their transformation from a wriggling, black comma beneath the water into a hopping, croaking, air-breathing frog?

Australia has a marvellous diversity of frogs, with around 220 different species. Compare that with 12 species in the whole of Europe and it's clear that Australia is a haven for frogs. Given the number of recent new findings, it's quite likely that there are new species of frogs yet to be discovered in remote parts of the country.

These days it isn't easy being green. Despite the large number of different species, our frogs are in trouble, with numbers considerably lower than they were a mere 20 years ago. Some species, particularly in tropical and sub-tropical areas, have become extinct. But even in New South Wales, for instance, about 25 per cent of the known species of frogs are considered 'at risk'.

The precise reasons for this decline aren't clear, though some scientists suspect that these amphibians are particularly susceptible to the pesticides and herbicides that have been widely used over the last few decades. Others point to

Building a habitat woodpile

If you have an open fire, a wood heater or even just a wood-fired barbecue, the chances are you store firewood in your garden. While collecting firewood can have harmful effects on animal habitats, you can give something back to the environment by using your woodpile as a shelter for all sorts of creatures in your habitat. Branches and logs can be piled up to provide shelter for all sizes of wildlife.

A shady spot is best for a habitat woodpile as it keeps the wood from drying out in the sun. By using different species of wood in the woodpile, you'll attract a wider variety of wildlife. Place the logs in criss-cross fashion first, then gradually build upward, using the largest logs at the bottom and smallest on top.

Your woodpile will probably attract fungi, the slow breakers-down of dead wood. Soon you'll also have spiders, beetles, wasps, lizards, slugs and snails, and then the birds and animals that make a meal of them. You could end up surprised at what comes to your woodpile, as we were one night when we found a fungus-loving potoroo coming to dine at ours.

global warming, seeing frogs as a kind of climatic change 'early warning system'. Another theory is the spread of a potentially fatal fungus moving among frog populations.

Whatever external and climatic pressures frogs are under, human beings, especially in urban areas, have added greatly to that pressure. We have radically altered habitats that used to suit frogs. Many creeks, marshes and ponds, necessary parts of an amphibian's habitat, have been drained, piped or covered in concrete.

The overall outcome is diminished healthy living space for frogs and fewer viable populations. In the garden it also means that we are far less likely to hear the once familiar sound of their croaking. While research into the frog decline continues to take place, it is possible for the habitat gardener to take part in their own small frog recovery program by turning backyards into refuges for these endearing but endangered creatures. The question is 'how?'

Attracting frogs to your garden is NOT as simple as collecting a few tadpoles from your local creek and plopping them into your pond. Firstly this may be illegal (regulations vary from state to state). Secondly you could find yourself introducing infection into the wild population (either from you when you collect, or from frogs that subsequently escape from your possibly infected pond or garden).

Even if you 'passively' attract frogs to your pond by providing ideal conditions for them, you should still be responsible for keeping frog hygiene in mind.

Frogs have a couple of basic needs.

Water is the major one. Frogs' skins are not waterproof, so most of them must have a permanent supply of water to keep their skin moist. If your garden lacks a water feature, whether natural or built, you are unlikely to attract and keep frogs. It is also vital to have a suitable supply of food for the frogs at every stage of their lifecycles: aquatic food for tadpoles; airborne and aquatic invertebrates for frogs. Spaces for shelter and breeding are also very important.

Once you have established that you can provide for the basic needs of frogs in your habitat garden, you need to know which species are likely to live and thrive in your local area. This isn't always as simple as it sounds. Frogs are not usually

The frog we love to hate

Not all frogs are welcome in the habitat garden. *Bufo marinus*, better known as the cane toad, is a blight on the Australian environment, and one that grows more serious by the year. Introduced in 1935 from South America, the cane toad was supposed to eat an introduced pest, the cane beetle. Instead it took to our native animals, devouring invertebrates, other amphibians and even small mammals, as well as poisoning many more. Cane toads have spread from Queensland into the Northern Territory and northern New South Wales, and are steadily moving south. If you live in an area infested with toads they could wreak havoc in your habitat garden. Contact FATS (the Frog and Tadpole Study Group) or your local Environment Department or National Parks and Wildlife Service for further information on how to deal with these dangerous pests.

active and visible during daylight hours, so you won't see them easily. Visually identifying them may take a lot of patience. Find a field guide for your area; these are usually available from local bookstores or newsagents.

A better bet is to try and identify local frogs by their call. Most frogs have quite distinctive calls. You may be able to identify them via written descriptions found in field guides (for example, the Eastern Banjo Frog has a banjo-like call that is sometimes written as 'pobble bonk'), but if you find this difficult, there are often recordings of frog calls available for different regions (on CD or audio cassette). Some frog calls can also be heard on the Internet. For instance, all Tasmanian frogs can be heard at the Parks and Wildlife website: www.parks.tas.gov.au/wildlife/frogs/frogs.html, while South Australian frog calls are found at the Environment South Australia website: www.environment.sa.gov.au/epa/frogcensus/frog_key.html. The Victorian Frogs Group includes a comprehensive location and call key on their website: www.frogs.org.au/frogs/location.html.

Not all frogs are suited to backyard ponds. To check which species are likely to thrive, contact the Frog and Tadpole Study Group (FATS) at PO Box A2405, Sydney South, NSW 2001 for further information. You could also check if this information is available from your local Environment Department or National Parks and Wildlife Service.

Tadpole and frog keeping essentials

After you've established whether you can legally introduce tadpoles into your backyard pond, or you've waited for them

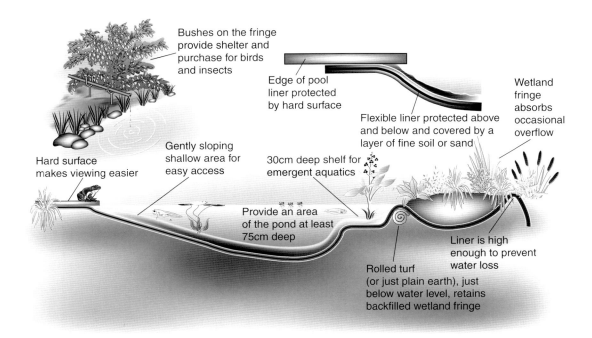

Design elements to consider when making a frog pond.

to find it of their own accord, the next step is finding out how to care for them.

Water

Chlorinated and highly oxygenated water is not good for tadpoles. If your tap water is treated with chlorine, it should stand for 1 to 5 days in a clean container to allow the chlorine to dissipate. Water gushing from taps and hoses is usually under pressure and inclined to be over-oxygenated. This should also be allowed to stand for at least a few hours to prevent tadpoles from absorbing too much oxygen, and becoming too buoyant. If you're using a pump to recycle water, or have an artificial waterfall in you pond, try to allow water to trickle rather than plunge into the pool which can also over-oxygenate it.

A frog pond should not be situated in full sun. Depending on where you are, as much as 75 per cent of the pond should be in shade most of the time, although some sunshine is important for the growth of algae. Shade can be provided by planting a variety of clumping plants and small shrubs close to the pond, and taller plants further away. A few leaves falling in the pond is fine, it even provides food for the tadpoles. Be careful of having too many leaves in the pond as they can supply too much nutrient and lead to algal growth which will smother the pond. If you have a small pond, and no filter or recirculation system, you will need to check and change the pond water from time to time. Try to do this before the water becomes cloudy or too dirty.

Food

Tadpoles feed on rotting organic matter, such as dead plant material, dead micro-organisms and even their own faeces. In the early stages you can supplement their food by introducing frozen lettuce, endive or similar leafy plant matter to the pond. Freezing the food material makes it easier for the tadpoles to digest it as it breaks down the plant cell walls. Be sure to thoroughly wash any vegetable matter before feeding it to tadpoles. They are very sensitive to any residual pesticides or herbicides that may be present. As well as being a means of you storing their food, freezing helps break the material into suitably small chunks. This is better than boiling the plant, which leaches some of the nutrients out of it. Native water plants

Dealing with mosquitos in your frog pond

It is NOT true that tadpoles will take care of any mosquito larvae in your pond. In fact they are rarely able to catch and eat live wrigglers. Frogs, which are mainly carnivorous, may do better with flying mozzies, but if you really want to get rid of mosquitos you're going to need fish. However most fish, even small native fish, are also rather partial to tadpoles. It is worth taking the trouble to find out which species of native fish can co-exist with tadpoles, while devouring mosquitos. In eastern Australia, for instance, the Pacific Blue-eye (*Pseudomugil signifer*), the White Cloud Mountain Minnow and the Fly-specked Hardyhead (*Craterocephalus stercusmuscarum fulvus*) are suitable companion fish. In the coastal southeast, the Australian Smelt (*Retropinna semoni*) is another example. Check with FATS or a similar group in your area for the best local native fish species for frog ponds.

are also a source of food and shelter for the tadpoles. Choose the particular species with great care. Any old pond weed will definitely NOT be suitable. Some weed species, such as water hyacinth and *salvinia*, have the capacity to escape from ponds and devastate local dams and waterways. Get advice from the Frog and Tadpole Study Group (FATS) or a similar group in your area.

Other habitat-friendly ways of dealing with mosquitos include:
- using a pump to circulate water in your pond. This makes the water less appealing to wrigglers, and also helps keep water quality higher;
- attracting wriggler-eating invertebrates, such as dragonflies (whose larvae eat wrigglers);
- attracting mosquito-eating birds, such as swallows, and mammals, such as bats.

Pond design

The broader issues of pond design for the habitat garden are in the multipurpose garden pond section on pp. 72–73. But when it comes to ensuring that the multipurpose pond is also frog-friendly, there are a few special features to bear in mind. As tadpoles develop front legs they need to be able to crawl out of the pond, so it should not be steep-edged. Make sure a ramped graduated shallow area is a part of the pond. If you are building your own pond, simply include this feature in the design. If you have purchased a ready-made pond, you can create a 'shallow end' using rocks, sand, logs or a mixture of natural material. It is also helpful for tadpoles and frogs to have some refuge, under either rock or vegetation, while still in the water.

Reptiles

Peoples' love of reptiles is usually very selective. Put simply, most of us love lizards but hate snakes. Venom is the main reason for this difference in affection towards snakes and lizards. Nevertheless snakes perform a vital role in the environment as one of the few native predators and scavengers

Snakes are part of most Australian habitats, so the habitat gardener shouldn't be surprised if a snake or two comes looking for a meal, a mate or a nest in their healthy habitat garden. On the other hand snakes are very shy and reclusive, so they may avoid a busy garden, or else make themselves scarce when you are present.

If you do discover them in your garden *you should not try to handle snakes yourself.* Most bites occur when people try to kill or handle snakes. Apart from that snakes are protected in most states and territories, so it is illegal to interfere with them. Most states have reptile rescue services, people who are expert at handling snakes. Contact your local Environment Department or National Parks and Wildlife Service for details.

Making a lizard garden

There are five different families of reptiles that come under the name 'lizards'. They are skinks, geckos, legless lizards, goannas and dragons. Lizards are found virtually everywhere in the world, with the exception of extremely cold places such as the Arctic and Antarctic. This is because lizards require some background warmth to keep their metabolic rate high enough to stay mobile. As a rule of thumb they can be expected not to be active below

15°C. This means that every part of Australia attracts some species of lizards.

Local lizards can be attracted to your garden as long as you meet a few of their basic needs. These include:
- shelter;
- food;
- water;
- warmth;
- protection from poisons and pets.

Here are some ways of providing these in your garden.

Shelter
In the wild, lizards often shelter in dense vegetation and ground debris, beneath bark, leaf litter, rocks, logs and log fragments. Leave plenty of groundcover in the garden. Where there is mulch, try to vary the depth and texture of the mulch, by throwing some large bark pieces and the occasional hollowed log onto the mulch. Groundcover or clumping plants, such as *Poa* and *Lomandra*, make ideal shelter and hide the invertebrate prey that some species of lizard feed on.

Food
Lizards are omnivorous, although most species tend towards being carnivorous. This means they'll feed on plant material such as fruit or vegetable matter but they generally prefer invertebrates, such as grubs, beetles, slugs and snails or small mammals and other reptiles. Their precise diet depends on their size and species. Lizards also tend to be opportunistic feeders, taking advantage of what's available and making a feast of it. Blue-tongue lizards, among others, have been known to steal canned pet food from the dog or cat's bowl, while goannas and some dragons will eat eggs. Most lizards find their food at ground level but some species, including goannas and dragons, may seek food in trees. In the habitat garden, a healthy layered garden will be sure to provide lizards with some of their food requirements. There's certainly no need to leave pet food out for them.

Water
A garden pond or any other reliable form of water at ground level will do fine for lizards in the garden.

Warmth
Lizards benefit from an additional heat source, so the provision of warm spaces in the garden is a must.

Any surface that is exposed to the sun for a few hours a day will do. Usually this will be rocks or logs, although walls, paths and steps are also used by heat-seeking lizards.

Protection from poisons and pets
Pesticides, herbicides, even chemical fertilisers can all harm lizards, especially omnivores such as blue-tongue lizards. Because lizards are near the top of the garden food chain, any chemicals used in your garden can end up concentrated in their bodies. Something as harmless as putting out snail bait could end up poisoning a blue-tongue, cutting short a lifespan that can be as long as 30 years.

Dogs and cats are also a major threat to lizards. Cats stalk and kill skinks; dogs are more likely to have a go at larger, slower-moving lizards like blue-tongues. Keeping your pets in at night will help, but controlling where they are and what they're doing by day is far more important. Provide pet-proof safe havens in the habitat garden, either with thick bushes or large log hollows, to protect lizards from all kinds of predators.

Australia's favourite lizard – the blue-tongue
These lizards are the largest members of the skink family (*Scincidae*), and possibly the most docile. Blue-tongue lizards have made quite a comfortable transition from their native bushland into urban backyards. The three most common blue-tongue lizards on the east coast of Australia are the Eastern Blue-tongue (*Tiliqua scincoides*), the Blotched Blue-tongue (*Tiliqua nigrolutea*) and the Shingleback (*Tiliqua rugosa*).

By being aware of the Blue-tongue lizard's natural habitat, it is possible to re-create the sort of environment that will attract it. This has many benefits for the habitat gardener, one of them being a decrease in snail populations – which are a favourite 'Bluey' snack.

Blue-tongues also eat many plant-eating insects. The blue-tongue's natural habitat is open country with plenty of ground-cover, for example, tussocky grasses and leaf litter. At night, they shelter in leaf litter or under large objects on the ground such as logs and rocks. As they are cold-blooded, blue-tongues must rely on the warmth of their environment to maintain their body temperature of 30–35°C. During the early morning blue-tongue lizards will often be seen basking in the sun. In the warmer parts of the day, they forage for food.

During cold weather blue-tongues will remain hidden and inactive in their shelter sites.

Blue-tongues have a diverse menu. Shinglebacks eat more plant matter than other species. Any animal matter that is eaten by blue-tongue lizards is generally of the slow-moving variety as they are not the speediest of hunters. However, blue-tongues do have large teeth and a strong jaw, which makes beetles and snails easy targets.

If threatened, a blue-tongue lizard will face its predator, open its mouth wide and stick out its blue tongue. If this behaviour does not repel the predator, the lizard may hiss and flatten out its body in an attempt to look larger. A frightened blue-tongue may bite if handled. This bite can be painful as it will break and bruise the skin but there is no venom present, so no long-term effects should be expected. If you are bitten, the bite should be cleaned with an antiseptic solution and covered.

In a skink-like manoeuvre, young blue-tongue lizards may drop the tip section of their tail if handled roughly by it. The stump will heal very quickly and the tail will slowly regenerate, although the loss of fat stored in the tail can weaken the animal.

In native bush, predators of the blue-tongue include large predatory birds, for example, Brown Falcons, Laughing Kookaburras; large snakes such as the Eastern Brown Snake, Red-bellied Black Snake and Mulga Snake, and cats and dogs. It is a good idea to keep pets in check if you wish to attract blue-tongue lizards to your habitat garden.

Aquatic animals

Running water is a joy, and always presents the architect or gardener with an opportunity for celebration; the dance to make something beautiful.
FROM 'WATERLOG' BY ROGER DEAKIN.

The multipurpose garden pond

Birds, mammals, amphibians, reptiles, insects, just about all living things, are to some extent reliant on water. The presence of a *permanent* water supply, not just an occasional supply, will help to attract local species to your garden, and keep them there. One way of keeping sources of water in the garden is to construct a multipurpose garden pond that's suitable for most of the water needs of a wide range of animals.

While there are many different ways to design ponds, some features are essential.

Permanent water supply

Drought is a regular feature of the Australian landscape so it is important to protect your habitat animals from the worst effects of water shortage. A permanent water supply provides a refuge and breeding ground for a countless number of species, and can be considered as a benign interference.

Fresh water always

As with birdbaths, water can be the source of cross-infection for animals. By keeping water fresh you will minimise the risk of such infection. A simple trickle of water into one end of the pond works well. The outflow at the lowest part of the pond can be planted out with local water-loving or bog plant species. Alternatively a return pump can be used to recirculate water.

These can be switched on with an automated timer system so they don't need to run all day and they can operate even when you're away. Solar-powered pumps are now available, and eliminate the need for an expensive and potentially hazardous connection to mains power.

Protection and shade

All the animals that use the pond will need protection of some sort, either from the weather or from predators. Water-loving grasses, reeds or other clumping foliage are best planted right next to the pond. These plants will provide refuge and possible food sources for small birds, frogs and insects. Rocks and mulch can also provide cover for some animals. Taller bushes and small trees, slightly further away, will provide shadow for the pond and perches for birds and insects.

Varying water depth

Start by considering the needs of all users of your pond. Birds might bathe in it, tadpoles could crawl out of it, insects may

---

Caution: children and garden ponds

If young children use or visit your garden take care where you place and how you design your garden pond. Children are naturally attracted to ponds and some protection will be necessary. If fencing the pond isn't practicable, consider attaching stout wire just above or below the surface of the pond. Cyclone wire or similar, if well anchored at the sides, should provide ample protection. It may also serve the secondary purpose of deterring fish-eating birds.

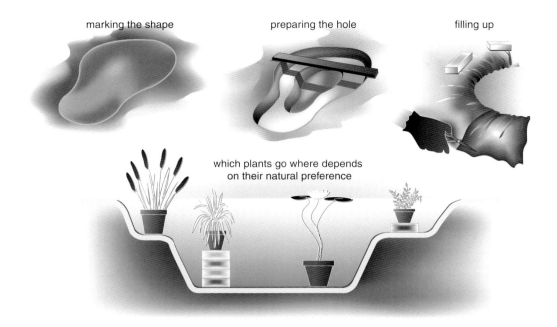

A simple do-it-yourself water garden design.

pupate at its edges, reptiles might drink from it, fish may swim in it. Each of these needs requires a slightly different pond depth or pond profile. Try to allow for these varying depths. If you design your own pond these can be taken into consideration before you construct it.

Another water depth consideration to take into account relates to seasonal variations in water levels. If you live in a part of Australia which has distinct wet and dry seasons, including many tropical and 'Mediterranean' climatic areas, you may want to consider allowing parts of your pond area to dry out during the dry season. This can be achieved by a combination of varied pond depths and varied water input levels.

Carefully choose your pond inhabitants

Whether it's fish, plants or some other life form that you want in your pond, you should choose them with care. Some species have a way of dominating their environment to the exclusion of other species. Carp, for example, take over from all other aquatic species including native fish and tadpoles and become the dominant species. In different parts of Australia certain aquatic plants have a similar capacity to dominate. *Salvinia*, alligator weed and water hyacinth are three examples, though other noxious species will vary from region to region. Typically such aquatic weeds have the capacity to form dense mats that eventually deplete the oxygen in the pond, causing it to stagnate. They can also be spread from your pond to the wider environment by birds and other animals. Check with your local Environment Department to find out which species should be avoided. Better still, seek out only local native plant and animal species for your pond.

Some aquatic and water-loving native plants

This list contains species from all around Australia. *Aquatic plants can become very invasive. Use only those species which occur naturally in your area.*

Section 1: Plants that generally prefer living in the water

Species Name	Common Name/s	Species Name	Common Name/s
Alisma plantago-aquatica	water plantain	*Limnophila australis*	
Aponogetum elongetus		*Ludwigia adscendens* and *Peploides* subsp. *Montevidensis*	
Azolla filiculoides and *pinnata*			
Ceratophyllum demersum	fox tail	*Lythrum salicaria*	purple loosestrife
Ceratopteris thalictroides	water sprite	*Marsilea* species	nardoo
Crassula helmsii		*Myriophyllum* species	water milfoils
Damasonium minus		*Nelumbo nucifera*	lotus
Elatine gratioloides		*Nymphaea* species	water lilies
Eleocharis acuta and *sphacelata*	spikerush	*Nymphoides* species	marshworts
		Ottelia species	
Gratiola peruviana		*Persicaria attenuata* and *decipiens*	knotweed
Hydrilla verticillata	water thyme		
Hygrophila angustipholia		*Potamogeton* (local species)	pondweeds
Ipomoea aquatica		*Triglochin* species	water ribbons
Isolepis fluitans and *subtilissima*		*Utricularia australis*	yellow bladderwort
		Vallisneria gigantea	ribbon weed, eel grass
Lemna minor	common duckweed	*Villarsia* species	

Building a habitat water garden

There's considerable choice in the kinds of water gardens and ponds you can use in the habitat garden, but generally there are three main options:
- have it custom-built;
- put in a ready-made pond;
- build it yourself.

With the first option, money willing, the choice of design and materials is up to you. Make sure the main features of a good water garden are taken into account when it is being built.

Ready-made ponds come in an astounding range of sizes and types. Most of them seem to be made of fibreglass or plastic and are coated with various substances to make them look more natural. These ponds do the job very well, although

Some aquatic and water-loving native plants (cont.)

Section 2: Plants that like wet feet, but not prolonged submersion

Species Name	Common Name/s	Species Name	Common Name/s
Adiantum species	maidenhair ferns	*Isotoma fluviatilis*	swamp ilsotome
Alpinia species	native gingers	*Lepidosperma gladiatum*	sword rush
Banksia robur	banksia	*Lomandra* species	sagg, mat rush
Baumea articulata	twig rush	*Mimulus* species	monkey flowers
Blechnum species	water ferns	*Oreobolus distichus*	
Callatriche Muelleri		*Philydrum lanuginosum*	
Carex species	tassell sedges	*Phragmites australis*	common reed
Centrolepis strigose		*Polystichum proliferum*	mother shield-fern
Cotula species	waterbuttons	*Pratia* species	pratia
Cyclosorua interruptus		*Ranunculus* (local species)	buttercups
Cyperus species		*Restio* species (some variously renamed as *Baloskion, Acion, Saropsis, Eurychorda*, etc)	cord rush
Danthonia nivicola			
Dawsonia superba	giant moss		
Drosera species	sundew (some species)	*Schoenoplectus* species	club rush
Epilobium pallidiflorum	willowherb	*Schoenus* species	
Gahnia species	saw sedge, cutting grass	*Todea barbara*	king fern
Hypericum japonicum		*Viminara juncea*	native broom
Isolepis hookeriana and *inundata*			

it is worth noting that many ready-made ponds lack the shallow ends or ledges that are so beneficial for frogs and semi-aquatic species. You can get around this by placing a rock or similar at the edge of the pond.

If you're going to build your own pond, follow a plan along the following suggestions:

Choose the site
A low-lying area that is already damp makes a lot of sense. Your pond should have a mixture of shade and some sun. For frogs, 60 to 70 per cent shade is ideal. Shade from shrubs and small trees is preferable to large overhanging trees, which may drop too many leaves.

Make the shape
Use a garden hose or length of string to form your outline shape. Mark out the shape using flour or chalk.

Dig the hole
Dig the hole, evenly at first, with a maximum depth of between 30cm and 50cm. Keep a horizontal line for the top of the pond, using a string or plank, plus a spirit level. This is especially important if your pond is on sloping ground. Otherwise the pond will constantly overflow. Once the hole is established, dig the side shelves, and make any other depth variations you want – bearing in mind that an even bottom is easier for placing pots or pumps on. Once the shape is right, compact the base material and remove any sharp rocks or roots that might puncture the pond liner. You can lessen the vulnerability of such materials to puncture by first lining the pond with carpet or pre-soaked cardboard or even a thick layer of newspaper.

Line the hole
There are many ways of lining the pond, but specialised heavy-duty pond lining material is widely available, and the best to use if you want to keep the water in. Lay the liner out over the hole, allowing plenty of overlap at the edges, before cutting with a sharp blade or scissors. Fold the overlap double to make a waterproof lip.

Fill the pond
Weigh the edges of the liner down with rocks, bricks or logs. Fill the pond slowly, allowing water to stretch the liner into place. Once it is filled use logs, rocks or cement to secure the edges of the liner in place. If you want a water-side observation area, consider using a large slab of rock, or put in treated pine mini-deck or paved area.

Pumps and filters
A circulating pump makes the water less attractive to mosquitos and helps slow the buildup of algae. A filter should not be necessary but it can be allowed for on the suction inlet of the submersible pump. If the pond is remote from a power source, or you're concerned with both safety and saving energy, you can install a solar-powered pump.

Finish off
Cover the bottom of the pond with washed gravel. Place rocks and logs in various places in and around the pond. These will become refuges and climbing posts for various species.

Plant out
When everything else is finished, and the water has been standing long enough to be the right temperature, and free of chlorine, you can start planting out and stocking the pond.

6. Special cases – habitat gardening in difficult zones

Despite its description as the 'wide brown land', Australia is a vast and complex country and there are literally hundreds of major climate and soil variations. That's one of the reasons we have such extraordinary biodiversity, and one of the reasons every habitat garden will be different.

There are particular zones, straddling many parts of Australia, which present special challenges to the habitat gardener. This chapter discusses the characteristics of each zone and looks at ways to achieve balanced habitat gardens.

Coastal gardens

Most Australians live close to the coast. And coastal gardening, whether in the tropics or the roaring forties, presents common challenges to the habitat garden.

Salt

Salt-laden winds are the most common difficulty in coastal gardens. When selecting plants for a coastal garden you must either choose salt-tolerant plant species (see list below), or protect plants from salty winds by using windbreaks. Windbreaks can be either natural, using plantings of salt-tolerant species, or artificial, using a screen, wall or barrier made from building materials, a brush fence, or similar.

Sand

Most coastal gardens also have to cope with sandy soils. While these drain very well, the downside is that they neither retain moisture nor nutrient well. Working on the principle that local conditions are what you live with in a habitat garden, large-scale changes to those soil conditions should be avoided. However if some increase in soil moisture and nutrient-retention properties is sought, this can be achieved by the use of such techniques as mulching, the application of (local) seaweed and the installation of a dripper watering system. Also watering in the early part of the day will help minimise moisture loss through evaporation.

Wind

Most of Australia's coastal areas are prone to afternoon sea breezes. The drying effects of these winds can add to water loss but also increase the detrimental effects of salt in the coastal garden. Protection from wind can be achieved by using windbreaks. Many of the salt-tolerant species listed on p. 78 are suitable for these types of plantings. If they do their job, the rest of the garden will be much less affected by salt, and you may be able to introduce a wider variety of plants into the protected zones.

The idea with a windbreak is not to create a complete wind barrier via a solid

A selection of salt-tolerant native plants

This list contains species from all around Australia. In a habitat garden use only those species that occur naturally in your area.

Species Name	Common Name/s	Species Name	Common Name/s
Acacia species (including *aulococarpa, cyclops, longifolia sophorae, suaveolens*)	wattle	*Hibiscus tiliaceus*	hibiscus
		Lagunaria patersonia	Norfolk Island hibiscus
		Leptospermum species (including *juniperinum, laevigatum* and *rotundifolium*)	tea trees
Agonis flexuosa	agonis		
Allocasuarina species (including *littoralis, verticillata*) and also *Casuarina equisetifolia*	she-oak	*Melaleuca* species (including *armillaris, halmaturorum,* and *lanceolata*)	paperbark, honey myrtles
Banksia species (including *integrifolia, serrata, spinulosa*)	banksia	*Olearia* species (including *axillaris, glutinosa* and *tomentosa*)	daisy bushes
Callitris gracilis	cypress pine		
Correa species	correa, native fuschia	*Paraserianthes lophantha*	albizia
Dianella tasmanica	flax lily	*Syzigium* species (including *australe, forte* and *oleosum*)	lilly pillies
Eucalyptus species (including *gummifera, platypus,* and *lehmannii*)	gum trees		
Hakea drupacea	hakea	*Westringia fruticosa*	coast rosemary
Hibbertia species (including *impetrifolia, scandens, vestita*)	hibbertia, guinea flower		

'wall' of plants. If a strong wind hits such a barrier it rises over it, creating a turbulent down-draught on the far side. This can damage plants and whatever else is beyond the barrier more than the original wind would have. A layered planting of salt-tolerant species of various heights and densities, with gaps between and around the plants, should do enough to break up the destructive force of most coastal winds.

Rainforest gardens

The usual image of rainforest is of a steaming tropical jungle. So it surprises some people to learn that pockets of rainforest are found in every Australian state and territory except South Australia. As the name implies, rainforest occurs naturally in areas that receive copious rainfall, usually upwards of 1500mm annually, though perhaps less in temperate areas. It also requires that the rainfall be

(continued page 80)

The Jewelled Spider (*Gasteracantha minax*) spins webs between shrubs in woodlands right across Australia, but especially near water. They feed on flying insects and can grow to the size of a 20 cent piece. (*Peter Tonelli*)

A dewy web – a beautiful sight even to arachnophobes, and a sign of a healthy habitat.

A Red-back Spider with egg sacs. A common and venomous spider, it thrives in sheds and rubbish piles that are left undisturbed. (*Peter Tonelli*)

The Eastern Banjo Frog (*Limnodynastes dumerili*), sometimes known as the 'pobblebonk', has a distinctive call. One frog's musical call of 'bonk' is replied to by another, with the resulting sound something like a plucked banjo. They prefer being near permanent water but will venture into gardens and across roads in wet weather. (*Peter Tonelli*)

The Large Green and Gold Frog (*Litoria raniformis*) is found across southeastern Australia, where it prefers well-vegetated areas near permanent water. Its call is a complex mixture of grunts and growls. (*Peter Tonelli*)

The call of the Brown Tree Frog (*Litoria ewingi*) – a repeated 'reeee-ree-ree-ree....' – is one of the common night sounds in gardens of Victoria and Tasmania. These small, agile frogs commonly breed in garden ponds, sheltering by day in thick vegetation or under rocks and logs. (*Peter Tonelli*)

A Spotted Marsh Frog (*Limnodynastes tasmaniensis*), common in both wooded and cleared areas of southeastern Australia. Its call is a repeated sharp 'click', resembling the clash of stones. (*Peter Tonelli*)

Striped Marsh Frogs (*Limnodynastes peroni*) are found throughout eastern and southern Australia. They prefer permanent water or wetlands with fringing vegetation. The male's call, a soft repeated 'whuck', is made from the safety of the water or concealed sites, such as under leaf litter. (*Peter Tonelli*)

Eastern Bearded Dragons are quite at home near human habitats, although they are vulnerable to attack from dogs and cats. These dragons can grow to 50cm in length, and are widespread throughout eastern Australia. (*Alex Dudley*)

Skinks seek out sunny rocks and logs, preferably near easy-to-find groundcover.

One of Australia's favourite reptiles is the blue-tongue lizard. This omnivorous skink will eat fruit, snails, and even stolen pet food. It's at home in the suburbs, but is threatened by our pets and our use of chemicals. (*Peter Tonelli*)

This Slender Blue-tongue is not directly related to the more familiar blue-tongue lizard. (*Peter Tonelli*)

Even in low rainfall areas, colourful plants such as Sturt's Desert Pea (*Swainsona Formosa*) can thrive.

Helichrysum put on a spectacular show in a favourable season.

Delightful splashes of colour such as from this wax flower (*Philotheca*) can often surprise the habitat gardener. (Ian Jeanneret)

A selection of native plants suitable for rainforest gardens

This list contains species from all around Australia. In a habitat garden, use only those species that occur naturally in your area. Most plants in Section 2 of the 'Aquatic Plants' list on pp. 74–75, would also be suitable for a rainforest garden.

Species Name	Common Name/s	Species Name	Common Name/s
Acacia melanoxylon	blackwood	*Gaultheria appressa*	wax berry
Acmena smithii	lilly pilly	*Lepiderema pulchella*	small-leaved tuckeroo
Acronychia oblongifolia		*Livistona* species	cabbage tree palms
Anopterus macleayanus	Macleay laurel, Queensland laurel	*Macadamia tetraphylla*	macadamia nut
		Melicope elleryana	corkwood
A. glandulosus	Tasmanian laurel	*Morinda jasminoides*	sweet morinda
Archontophoenix alexandrae	Alexander palm	*Mucuna gigantean*	burny bean
		Murraya ovatifoliolata	mock orange
A. cunninghamiana	Bangalow palm, piccabeen	*Nothofagus cunninghamii*	myrtle, myrtle beech
Asplenium australasicum	bird's nest fern	*Pandorea jasminoides*	bower of beauty
Austromyrtus species		*P. pandorana*	Wonga-wonga vine
Backhousia myrtifolia	carrol, grey myrtle	*Passiflora* species	
Baloghia inophylla	scrub bloodwood	*Phyllocladus aspleniifolius*	celery-top pine
Billardiera longiflora		*Piper novae-hollandiae*	native pepper
Blechnum species	water ferns	*Pothos longipes*	native pothos
Brachychiton discolor	lacebark	*Ptychosperma elegans*	solitaire palm
B. acerifolius	flame tree	*P. macarthurii*	MacArthur palm
Calanthe triplicata	Christmas orchid	*Randia* species	gardenias
Cissus antarctica	water vine, kangaroo vine	*Sloanea australis*	maiden's bush
		S. woollsii	yellow carabeen
C. hypoglauca	water vine	*Stenocarpus sinuatus*	firewheel tree, wheel of fire
Cyathea species	tree-ferns		
Dianella species	flax lilies	*Syzigium* species (including *erythrocalyx*, *moorei* and *wilsonii*)	lilly pillies
Dicksonia antarctica	soft tree-fern, man fern		
Doryphora sassafras	sassafras	*Tetrastigma nitens*	shining grape
Eucryphia species	leatherwood	*Tristaniopsis laurina*	water gum
Faradaya splendida	potato vine	*Viola hederacea*	native violet

fairly regular, that there is no dry season, and that soil and other site conditions be suitable. Parts of western and central Tasmania; parts of highland and coastal Victoria, Queensland and New South Wales; and pockets of the Northern Territory and Western Australia are rainforest areas.

Rainforest also needs to be left uncleared for a sufficient time in order to develop. While it once covered a much larger area, landclearing and logging have reduced it to only around 0.3 per cent of Australia's land surface. In many cases the surviving rainforest is in isolated pockets, a situation which threatens its ongoing growth and health.

Fortunately, rainforests are some of the best-loved landscapes on earth, and many gardeners are at the forefront of the movement wanting to save them. In the right setting, this desire can translate into the re-creation of patches of rainforest in our backyards, leading to an overall extension of their spread. There are particular issues and considerations involved in creating a habitat rainforest garden as follows:

Water
While it is perfectly possible to re-create a rainforest in any garden setting, provided you keep the water up to the plants, the principles of habitat gardening ask that you favour local species. This means that you would only grow a rainforest habitat garden in an area that is in a high rainfall zone that is, or once was, suitable for rainforest species.

Of course it may be that a wetter section of a garden in a drier, non-rainforest area would make an ideal setting for a rainforest niche. Here the main considerations would remain (a) the use of local plant species, and (b) care with the use of additional water.

Plant selection
There is no special magic that makes a plant a 'rainforest plant'. It is simply a plant that can and does grow in rainforest settings, even if it also thrives in other settings. The fern *Dicksonia antarctica* is a good example. While it's found in rainforests from Tasmania to Queensland, it can thrive in any reasonably damp and sheltered setting.

In choosing plants for a rainforest habitat garden you should follow the same general guidelines as for any other habitat garden, that is, start by favouring the locals. As you may not have true rainforest in your neighbourhood, you could start by seeing what grows in the wettest parts of your local area or contacting your local nursery.

Arid and semi-arid gardens
Much of inland Australia, and sections of coastal Western Australia and South Australia, can be described as arid or semi-arid. The definition of arid or semi-arid is somewhat flexible. However the main ingredient is a lack of rainfall, either seasonally or over the whole year. Therefore the selection of suitable plants, usually those with a degree of drought tolerance, is crucial to the semi-arid habitat garden.

Nevertheless, it is also wise to help seedlings to become established by protecting them from drought for the first year or two. This can be achieved by watering, preferably before or after the

A selection of native plants for semi-arid areas

This list contains species from many of the drier parts of Australia. In a habitat garden use only those species that occur naturally in your area.

Species Name	Common Name/s	Species Name	Common Name/s
Acacia species (including *aneura, cooletioides, coriacea, deanei, decora, rubida, implexa, hakeoides, papyrocarpa, paradoxa, pendula* and *salicina*)	wattle	*Eremophila* species	emu bushes, poverty bushes
		Eucalyptus species (including *diversifolia, gracilis, grossa, kruseana, lansdowneana, microtheca, oleosa, orbifolia, papuana, tetragona, thozetiana* and *viridis*)	gum trees
Allocasuarina species (including *decaisneana, inophloia, luehmannii, nana* and *verticillata*)	she-oak	*Grevillea* species (including *dryandri, excelsior, floribunda insignis, intricate, juncifolia, pteridifolia,* and *wickhamii* subspecies *aprica*)	grevilleas
Brachyscome (various)	brachyscome, native daisies		
Banksia ornata	banksia		
Brachychiton rupestris	bottle tree	*Hakea* species (including *chordophylla, francisiana, muelleriana, purpurea* and *tephrosperma*)	hakea
Callitris gracilis	cypress pine		
Calotis cuneifolia	blue burr-daisy		
Casuarina cristata	belah	*Melia azedarach* var. *australasica*	white cedar
Chrysocephalum (various)	yellow buttons, paper daisies	*Themeda australis*	kangaroo grass
Dodonaea (various)	hop-bushes		

heat of the day, and/or through the application of mulch. In some areas salt in the soil is also a problem. The use of salt-tolerant species may be helpful here (see the table earlier in this chapter on p. 78).

Alpine and cool climate gardens

What's considered a cool climate in Australia is quite relative when compared with other parts of the world. Very few of us ever see snow in our gardens, and relatively few experience temperatures below 0°C. True alpine areas, those above the tree line, are rare in Australia. For instance, even in the cool, mountainous state of Tasmania only about 3 per cent of the land area is alpine, and very few people live permanently in such areas.

For the purposes of this section, the definition of a cool climate area is one which has either a significant number of frosts per year and/or has average daytime temperatures below 15°C for at least a couple of months per year. Typically the

A selection of native plants for alpine and cooler areas

This list contains species from a variety of alpine and cooler parts of Australia. In a habitat garden use only those species that occur naturally in your area.

Species Name	Common Name/s	Species Name	Common Name/s
Acacia species (including *aneura, boormanii, buxifolia, genistifolia, gunnii, melanoxylon, montana, obliquinervia* and *verticillata*)	wattle	*Diplarrena* (*moraea* or *latifolia*)	flag iris
		Eucalyptus species (including *cunninghamii, cinerea, crenulata, dives, gummifera, leucoxylon, mannifera, moorei, pauciflora, perriniana, polyanthemos, rossii* and *stricta*)	gum trees
Allocasuarina (various)	she-oak		
Baeckia (various)	baeckia		
Blechnum species (including *nudum* and *penna-marina*)	water-ferns		
		Goodenia (various)	goodenia
Banksia species (including *canei, integrifolia* and *marginata*)	banksia	*Grevillea* species (including *acanthifolia, australis, gaudichaudii, juniperina, repens* and *victoriae*)	grevillea
Brachyscome (various)	brachyscome, native daisies	*Hakea* (various)	hakea
Chionocloa pallida	wallaby grass	*Lomatia* (various)	lomatia
Chrysocephalum (various)	yellow buttons, paper daisies	*Melaleuca* (various)	paperbark
Dianella (various)	flax lilies	*Olearia* (various)	daisy bushes

combination of cool climate and alpine areas takes in the ranges and tablelands of eastern and southeastern Australia, and inland and higher parts of Tasmania.

Whichever way the definition goes, alpine and cooler climate areas have one thing in common: a significant amount of cold weather. But while frost and occasional snow may seem to be their public enemy Number One, there are other factors that can challenge gardeners in our cooler climes. Even in Australia's cooler areas, summers can often be hot and dry. Desiccating winds, whether hot or cold, are adverse conditions for gardens.

So the key factors to consider in these areas are usually:

Frost

Severe frost can limit germination and growth, kill sensitive plants and damage even frost hardy plants. This happens through the freezing and thawing of the fluids within the plants. The resulting expansion and contraction of the fluid as it solidifies can burst plant structures and prevent them from doing their job. If the damage is extensive the plant will die.

The use of frost resistant species, which have developed such mechanisms as narrow leaves, with a smaller surface area exposed to the cold, is a good ploy in colder areas. For species that are marginal to such areas, or vulnerable in their early stages, the presence of some form of temporary protection is a good precaution. Large protective structures – whether artificial, such as buildings or walls, or natural, such as larger plants or rock shelves – create a microclimate, which is often sufficient to protect vulnerable plants against cold during their early growth. Temporary protection of seedlings and young plants can also be achieved by covering them overnight with hessian, shadecloth or similar. However the main secret is to choose species which have a history of surviving the conditions in your area.

Water

Although alpine and cooler areas are often wet, it is seldom the case that too much water kills alpine plants. It is far more likely that a hot, dry spell over summer will cause problems. So it's wise to try and protect your younger plants from these dry spells. Where watering is not desirable or possible, the application of a thick mulch will help prevent the soil from drying out. Mulch can also temper the effects of frost by acting as a blanket that keeps soil temperatures higher.

Wind

Even frost hardy plants can be killed by constant wind, particularly if it is ice-laden in winter, or hot and dry in summer. Wind protection by means of a windbreak is advisable if such winds are common in your area. See pp. 77–78 for information on planting windbreaks.

Blossom burst — a time eagerly awaited by gardeners and wildlife alike. Here a Tasmanian blue gum begins flowering. (*Ian Jeanneret*)

7. Getting help

Although the cultivation of native plants in Australian gardens has been popular for many years, what we call habitat gardening is still relatively new in this country. Nonetheless there are many places and people to go to for help with your habitat garden.

Government/community environmental care groups

In virtually every part of Australia there are government and/or community-based environmental care groups such as Landcare, Bushcare and Greening Australia. The great value of these groups is the local nature of their expertise when it comes to your area. They are likely to know what sort of vegetation is or was endemic to your area. Beyond that they may also know where you can locally obtain such plants, and how to plant and nurture them.

In many cases you can also join in with the local projects of these groups. This will give you some expertise in bush regeneration, which you'll be able to transfer into your own garden. But it will also help you to contribute to habitat restoration beyond your property boundary. Here are some of the web contacts for some relevant organisations. In most cases they will be able to put you in touch with any active local group.

Greening Australia
www.greeningaustralia.org.au

Landcare
www.landcareaustralia.com.au

Bushcare
www.ea.gov.au/land/bushcare

Men of the Trees
www.menofthetrees.com.au (a WA site, but with links to other states)

Australian Bush Heritage
www.bushheritage.asn.au

Gardens for Wildlife
www.sef.org.au/gfw

Specialist gardens

Australia has well over 100 botanic gardens and arboreta covering virtually every corner of the country. These public gardens contain a wealth of ideas and information regarding gardening. All Australian botanic gardens, and many other public gardens, have at least some native Australian plants on display. While these gardens may not specifically help with your habitat gardening, you can often learn general lessons about native plantings.

There's now a trend worldwide for public gardens to also have wildlife-friendly plantings. I was surprised on a recent visit to the United Kingdom to find that even the late Queen Mother's gardens at St James Palace in the heart of London have a mowing regimen that allows meadow growth that's kind to local birds, mammals and insects.

Increasingly it's not just native species, but local native species that are being given special prominence. By visiting your nearest public garden you can learn which plants do well in your area, plus the conditions they seem to prefer. You may even find out details such as the kinds of animal or insect species they attract. Many public gardens also try to feature remnant native vegetation, bush that remains from before European settlement, within their grounds.

Here are just a few of Australia's gardens and arboreta, arranged state by state, that feature local native plantings and/or remnant native vegetation.

Queensland

Brisbane Botanic Gardens, Mt Coot-tha – contains a new 27-hectare section called 'Australian Plant Communities', which aims to display as wide a variety of Australian native plants as possible. It functions like a living library of plants, creating a window into the plant communities found in this part of Australia. Plants are grouped in communities: dry sclerophyll forest, heathland, wetland, sub-tropical rainforest and tropical rainforest.

Atherton Arboretum, Atherton – part of the CSIRO's Tropical Forest Research Centre, which includes 3 hectares of native plants.

Anderson Park, Townsville – a 27-hectare garden with substantial native plantings.

Flecker Botanic Gardens, Cairns – a large tropical garden, including wet tropics plants and a wetland feature. Directly adjacent is the Mt Whitfield Conservation Park, with over 300 hectares of natural forested slopes.

New South Wales and Australian Capital Territory

The National Botanic Gardens, Canberra, ACT – Australia's principal native garden, with local Canberra/Black Hill species given prominence. There's also a huge variety of species from all over Australia.

The Jervis Bay annexe of the National Botanic Gardens, Jervis Bay, NSW – local coastal species are given special prominence.

Mt Tomah Botanic Garden, Blue Mountains, NSW – a fine cool climate garden that includes many native plants.

Mt Annan Botanic Garden, near Campbelltown, NSW – this outlier of Sydney's Royal Botanic Garden is found in the outer southwest of the city. It contains many rare and endangered native plants, as well as valuable remnants of the grassy woodlands once common in the region.

Burrendong Arboretum, Mumbil, near Wellington, NSW – contains many drought-tolerant native plants.

Illawarra Grevillea Park, near Wollongong, NSW – has many hundreds of grevilleas plus a wide range of other natives. It also has a rainforest walk that displays a wealth of indigenous rainforest species.

Victoria
Royal Botanic Gardens, Melbourne – one of Australia's finest planted gardens; still has some remnant indigenous vegetation, notably along sections of the Yarra River and near the Observatory Gate. Other native plantings are also prominent.

Royal Cranbourne Botanic Gardens, Cranbourne – an outlier of the main Melbourne Gardens, these gardens cover 360 hectares of Australian bushland, some of it remnant indigenous bush. It is one of the best locations to enjoy the splendour and diversity of Australian flora.

Karwarra Australian Plant Garden, Lilydale – 100 per cent natives.

Tasmania
Royal Tasmanian Botanical Gardens, Hobart – a fine garden, with ample plantings of natives. A special feature adjacent to the Gardens is the remnant native grassland on the slopes of the Domain.

Tasmanian Bushland Garden, Buckland – a new 25-hectare garden featuring a mixture of species found in southeast Tasmania

South Australia
Mount Lofty Botanic Garden, near Adelaide – includes a self-guided nature trail that winds through 7 hectares area of natural scrub. Visitors can discover native plants and animals in a managed but natural setting.

Wittunga Botanic Garden, Fleurieu Peninsula – features plants from the Fleurieu Peninsula and Kangaroo Island, southern Western Australia, and includes a fine collection of eucalypts. Meandering pathways through the Terrace and Sandplain Gardens give visitors the opportunity to see these distinctive and colourful collections. Many different birds can be seen, attracted by the good supplies of nectar produced by the flowers of plants in the collection.

Western Australia
Kings Park and Botanic Gardens, Perth – a vast and remarkable urban park and botanic garden. It features West Australian species prominently, especially the brilliant wildflowers. But the Gardens also play a very special role in the conservation of Western Australia's unique local species, and local native plantings are prominent throughout.

Dryandra Woodland, Narrogin – this is one of the prime places in the southwest of Western Australia for viewing native wildlife and remnant woodland habitats. A predator-proof compound contains populations of many rare native species.

Kalgoorlie Arboretum, Kalgoorlie – has a wide variety of indigenous flora, including a remnant woodland area. They have 65 observed bird species, partly thanks to a small dam, and a stand of river gums (*Eucalyptus camaldulensis*).

Northern Territory

Darwin Botanic Gardens, Darwin – a diverse garden with an increasing focus on tropical northern Australian species, including a natural mangrove section and a monsoon forest gully.

Alice Springs Desert Park, Alice Springs – this cross between a garden and a wildlife park displays a wide variety of arid and semi-arid plants and animal species. Most are found in natural or reconstructed habitat zones, including grassland, woodland, floodplains and sandy desert.

Olive Pink Botanic Garden, Alice Springs, NT – is the most developed arid zone botanic garden in Australia. It has over 300 of Central Australia's plant species. Many of these are in areas of simulated habitat that reflect their natural occurrence. These habitats include a desert sand dune system, a mulga woodland, a rocky waterhole and a creek floodout. These are set below large rocky hills that carry naturally occurring vegetation. A number of rare and relict species are grown.

Societies and clubs

Many specialist groups and societies can help with particular areas of habitat gardening. Here are just a few with their national or main office contacts:

Australian Plant Society (nationally under the umbrella of the Association of Societies for Growing Australian Plants (ASGAP)
Web: http://farrer.riv.csu.edu.au/ASGAP/apoline.html (national site, with links to state societies)
Email: sgap@ozemail.com.au

Bird Observers Club of Australia
Phone: 1300 305 342 or (03) 9877 5342
Web: www.birdobservers.org.au
Email: boca@ozemail.com.au

Birds Australia
(formerly the Royal Australian Ornithological Union) 415 Riversdale Rd, Hawthorn East VIC 3123
Phone: (03) 9882 2622
Fax: (03) 9882 2677
Web: www.birdsaustralia.com.au
Email: mail@birdsaustralia.com.au

The Gould League
PO Box 1117
Moorabbin VIC 3189
Phone: (03) 9532 0909
Fax: (03) 9532 2860
Web: www.gould.edu.au
Email: gould@gould.edu.au

Wildlife Information and Rescue Service (WIRES)
Phone: (in NSW) 1800 641 188 or (Sydney) (02) 8977 3333
Web: www.wires.au.com (has links to similar groups elsewhere in Australia)

Frog and Tadpole Study Group (FATS)
PO Box 296
Rockdale NSW 2216
Web: www.fats.org.au (a NSW site, but with links to other states)
Email: fatsgroupnsw@hotmail.com

The Amphibian Research Centre (ARC)
PO Box 959, Merlynston VIC 3058
Phone: (03) 9354 4718
Fax: (03) 9306 9356
Web: www.frogs.org.au
Email: arc@frogs.org.au

World Wide Fund for Nature
PO Box 528
Sydney NSW 2001
Phone: (02) 9281 5515 or 1800 032 551
Fax: (02) 9281 1060
Web: www.wwf.org.au
Email: enquiries@wwf.org.au

Specialist nurseries

There's a continual increase in the number of nurseries specialising in growing and selling local species. The Australian Plant Society (APS) has issued a booklet called *Buy What Where?* which has an up-to-date list of nurseries as at May 2000. Contact the APS (details above) for further information.

The Indigenous Nurseries Network (in Vic.), part of the Indigenous Flora and Fauna Association, lists many Victorian specialist nurseries on their website. Go to http://home.vicnet.net.au/~iffa/nursery1.htm

Further reading – a brief selection that can be supplemented with books written for your local region

Plants
The Austraflora A–Z of Australian Plants by Bill Molyneux and Sue Forrester (Reed, 1998)
Australian Native Gardening – Made Easy by Dick Chadwick (Little Hills Press, 1985)
Australian Native Plants, 4th Edition, by John Wrigley and Murray Fagg (Reed, 1996)
Encyclopaedia of Australian Plants (multivolume) by Rodger Elliot and David Jones (Lothian, various dates)
Let's Propagate by Angus Stewart (ABC Books, 1999)

Wildlife
Attracting Birds to Your Garden in Australia by John Dengate (New Holland, 1997)
Attracting Butterflies to Your Garden by Densey Clyne (Reed, 2000)
Attracting Frogs to Your Garden by Kevin Casey (Kimberley Productions, 1996)
Attracting Wildlife to Your Garden by Rodger Elliot (Lothian, 1994)
The Australian Bird-Garden by Graham Pizzey (HarperCollins, 2000)
Complete Book of Australian Mammals by Ronald Strahan (ed.) (Angus & Robertson, 1991)
A Field Guide to Insects in Australia by Paul Zborowski and Ross Storey (Reed, 1995)
Tracks, Scats and Other Traces by Barbara Triggs (Oxford University Press, 1996)

General
The Bush Garden by Esther Wettenhall (Hyland House, 1995)
Creating a Wildlife Garden by Bob and Liz Gibbons (Chancellor Press, 1988)
Growing Locals by Robert Powell and Jane Emberson (WA Naturalists' Club, 1996)

Afterword

Imagine starting up a restaurant. Those first few months must be quite tense. Will the customers come? If they do, will they like what you have prepared? Will they keep coming and will they spread the word?

You may feel a bit like that novice restaurateur once you've got your habitat garden going. Will the birds and other animals come? Will it really work? While a certain amount of faith and optimism may seem in order, be encouraged. Your habitat garden has huge advantages over any restaurant.

Consider:

What opposition do you have?
Look around your neighbourhood. Is there already everything that an insect, bird or mammal could want from an environment?

What have you got to lose?
A habitat garden isn't going to send you bankrupt. But it just could make a big difference to the survival of some local species.

You can always make changes
as things do or don't work.

What are the rewards?
Just one flowering plant can make a huge difference to birds, invertebrates and even small mammals. Imagine the difference a whole habitat garden can make.

There are still other rewards that may flow from having a functioning habitat garden. You could:
- become more familiar with the behaviour and seasonal doings of 'your' plant and animal inhabitants and visitors;
- start photographing, drawing, painting or writing about what's going on in your habitat garden;
- get involved with nature conservation outside your garden boundary through wildlife rescue, habitat restoration or similar projects in your local area – and beyond.

In short you may find that this form of gardening, where you can make such positive contributions to our environment, is about as rewarding as it can get. Happy habitat gardening!

Index

alpine gardens, 81–83
amphibians, 65–69
animals
    amphibians, 65–69
    birds *see* birds
    insects, 58–65
    mammals *see* mammals
    reptiles, 69–71
ants, 59–60
aquatic animals, 72–76
aquatic plants, 74–75
arboreta, 85–88
arid gardens, 80–81

B
balancing habitats, 38
bandicoots, 52
bats, 52–53, 55, 69
bees, 50
biodiversity, 6
biological pest control, 39–40
bird feeders, 49
birdbaths, 46
birds
    attracting, 45–76
    feeding, 48–49
    food plants, 46
    hollow trees, 50
    nesting for, 47, 49
    predatory, 71
    problems, 50
    providing refuge, 47
    threats to, 47–48
    water, 46
    window hazards, 50
blue-tongue lizards, 39, 43, 70, 71
boiling water seed treatment, 18–23
botanic gardens, 85–88
brush fences, 77
bulldozed blocks, 14–16
bush rocks, 37
bush wildlife corridors, 15–16
bushes, 9–10, 54
bushfire risks, 27
butterflies, 58, 59, 60, 63

C
cane toad, 66
carp, 73
caterpillars, 24, 59–60
cats, 41, 48, 49, 54, 70
changes in your garden, 43–44
chemicals, 25, 39, 40, 47–48, 65, 68, 70
child-proof pond fencing, 72
chlorinated water, 68, 76
city gardens, 15
clay, 25
climatic factors, 12
climbers, 9
clubs, 88–89
clumping plants, 8, 54
coastal gardens, 77–78
coir peat, 23
complexone, 42
contouring, 25
controlled release fertilisers, 24
cool climate gardens, 81–83
cuttings, 17, 18

D
damsel flies, 62
desert gardens, 80–81
dieback, 38
difficult habitats, 77–83
direct seeding, 29
dogs, 70
dragonflies, 60–62, 69
drainage, 12, 77
drip watering, 11, 34
drought, 11, 33–34, 72, 80

E
earthworks, 25
ecological niches, 43

escaped plants and animals, 6
eucalypts, plantings near, 30–31
exotic plants, 15

F

fairy martins, 48
feed tables, 48–49
fences, brush, 77
feral plants and animals, 6
fertilisers, 24
fire, 26–27, 28, 38
fish, 68, 73
flying foxes, 55
food plants
    birds, 46
    flying foxes, 55
    koalas, 55
    mammals, 54
formal gardens, 15
frogs, 66–69
frost, 26, 82–83
fungus attacks on seedlings, 24

G

garden features as a lawn alternative, 35
genetic diversity, 18
glasshouses, 24
grasses, 8, 35
groundcovers, 8, 35
growing mediums for seed, 23
growth, 17–32
    suppressing, 36
gypsum, 25

H

hand weeding, 25
hardwood mulches, 36
help, 85–89
herbicides, 25, 65, 68, 70
hollow trees for wildlife, 50
honeybees, 50
house position, 13

I

insecticides, 39, 47–48, 65, 68, 70
insects, 58–65
invertebrates, 58–65

K

koala food plants, 55

L

large gardens, 29
lawn alternatives, 34–35
layered planting, 8–10
leaf loss, 40
lizards
    bites, 71
    blue-tongue, 39, 43, 70, 71
    feeding, 69–71
    gardens for, 69–71
    predatory birds, 71
    shinglebacks, 71
local animals and plants, 5–6, 26

M

magpie attacks, 50
maintenance, 33–44
mammals, 51–58
    attracting, 53–54
    benefits from, 51–52
    in ceilings, 57
    escaped, 6
    food plants, 53
    nesting materials, 54
    as pests, 55–58
    providing refuge, 54
    threats to, 54
    water, 54
mass plantings, 29
meadows, wildflower, 35
mesurol, 42
metaldehyde, 42
methiocarb, 42
mimicking nature, 6–7
mosquitos, 60, 68, 69, 76
moths, 58, 59, 63
mulching, 33–37
    difficult zones, 77
    frost-prone areas, 83
    hardwood, 36
    materials, 36–37
    new plantings, 36
    newspaper, 25
    organic, 34

planting out, 28
quantities, 35–36
reasons for, 35
site preparation, 25, 28

N

native animals *see* mammals
native birds *see* birds
native grasses as a lawn alternative, 35
native plants
    alpine and cool climate gardens, 82
    aquatic, 74
    to attract butterflies, moths, 62–65
    direct seeding, 29
    fertilisers, 24
    fire-hardy, 28
    nectar-rich, 46
    pruning, 37
    rainforest gardens, 79
    salt-tolerant, 78
    semi-arid gardens, 81
    shade-tolerant, 30–31
    swamp, 74
nectar-rich plants, 46
nesting boxes and materials
    birds, 47, 49
    mammals, 54
    possums, 55–56
noxious weeds, 41

O

organic mulches, 34
over-watering, 11
oxygenated water, 68

P

paving as a lawn alternative, 35
peat moss substitutes, 23
pest management, 11–12, 38–44
pesticides, 39, 47–48, 65, 68, 70
phosphorous fertilisers, 24
planning, 5–16
   basic questions, 11
   processes, 12–14
   reasons for, 12
plant propagation, 17–24
   see also seeds

   cuttings, 17, 18
   methods for selected plants, 19–22
   reasons for, 17
planting out
   mulching, 28
   near eucalypts, 30–31
   site preparation, 27–28
   watering, 28
planting times, 25–26
planting tubes, 23–24
plants
   density, 26
   escaped, 6
   fire-hardiness, 26–27
   mix, 26
   native *see* native plants
   propagation methods *see* plant propagation
   size, 26
   tolerating damage to, 40
plastic rubbish, 48
pond fencing, 72
ponds, 33, 46–47
possums, 52, 54, 55–58
predatory birds, 71
propagation *see* plant propagation
pruning native plants, 37–38
pumps, solar-powered, 72, 76

R

rainfall, 11, 12, 80
rainforest gardens, 78–80
rats, 49–50
Red-back spider, 64
regeneration after fire, 38
repellants, possum, 57–58
reptile rescue services, 69
reptiles, 69–71
runways, animal, 52

S

salt, 77–78, 81
salt-tolerance, 81
   native plants, 78
sandy soils, 77
sea breezes, 77–78
seedbeds, 29
seedlings, 24

seeds, 17–24
    abrasion, 22
    boiling water treatment, 18–23
    cooling, 23
    gathering your own, 18
    germinating alpines, 23
    germination, 18, 24
    getting, 17–18
    growing mediums, 23
    planting, 23
    smoke and smoke water treatment, 22–23
    sowing and growing medium, 23
    storage, 22
semi-arid gardens, 80–81
shade problems, 32
shade-tolerant native plants, 30–31
shinglebacks, 71
shrubs, 9–10, 54
site preparation, 12, 25
slugs, 24, 41–43, 71
small gardens, 15, 27
smoking seeds, 22–23
snails, 24, 41–43, 70, 71
snake bites, 69
snakes, 69
societies, 88–89
soil
    improvement, 25
    salt in, 81
    sandy, 77
solar-powered pumps, 72, 76
sowing mediums, 23
specialist gardens, help for, 85–89
specialist nurseries, 89
spiders, 62–65
storing seeds, 22
sugar gliders, 53
sunshine hours, 12
swallows, 48, 69
Sydney Funnel-web, 64

T

tadpoles, 65, 66–69
toads, 66

trees
    description and benefits, 10
    hollow, for wildlife, 50
    large, 26
    for small gardens, 27
tufting plants, 8

W

wasps, 50
water
    to attract birds, 46–47
    to attract mammals, 54
    conservation, 7–11, 33
    cross-infection, 47, 72
    plant stress, 32
water gardens, 74–76
watering
    alpine gardens, 83
    maintenance, 33–34
    planting out, 28
watering systems, 34
weed mats, 34
weeding, 25
weeds
    bird damage, 38–44
    identification, 40–41
    natural management, 11–12
    noxious, 41, 73
    site preparation, 25
    suppressing, 39
White-tailed spider, 64
wildflower meadows as a lawn alternative, 35
wildlife *see* animals
wildlife corridors in bushy areas, 15–16
wind
    alpine gardens, 83
    coastal gardens, 77–78
windbreaks, 77–78, 83
windows as bird hazard, 50–51
wombats, 52
woodpiles as wildlife habitats, 65